THE BEDFORD SERIES IN HISTORY AND CULTURE

# Hospital Sketches
## by Louisa May Alcott

Related Titles in
# THE BEDFORD SERIES IN HISTORY AND CULTURE
*Advisory Editors:* Natalie Zemon Davis, Princeton University
Ernest R. May, Harvard University
Lynn Hunt, University of California, Los Angeles
David W. Blight, Yale University

---

THE SOVEREIGNTY AND GOODNESS OF GOD *by Mary Rowlandson*
*with Related Documents*
Edited with an Introduction by Neal Salisbury, *Smith College*

*Judith Sargent Murray: A Brief Biography with Documents*
Sheila L. Skemp, *University of Mississippi*

*Margaret Fuller: A Brief Biography with Documents*
Eve Kornfeld, *San Diego State University*

*William Lloyd Garrison and the Fight against Slavery:*
*Selections from* THE LIBERATOR
Edited with an Introduction by William E. Cain, *Wellesley College*

*Women's Rights Emerges within the Antislavery Movement, 1830–1870:*
*A Brief History with Documents*
Kathryn Kish Sklar, *State University of New York at Binghamton*

*Abraham Lincoln, Slavery, and the Civil War: Selected Writings*
*and Speeches*
Edited by Michael P. Johnson, *Johns Hopkins University*

TWENTY YEARS AT HULL-HOUSE *by Jane Addams*
Edited with an Introduction by Victoria Bissell Brown, *Grinnell College*

*Women's Magazines, 1940–1960: Gender Roles and the Popular Press*
Edited with an Introduction by Nancy A. Walker, *Vanderbilt University*

# Hospital Sketches

## by Louisa May Alcott

*Edited with an Introduction by*

## Alice Fahs

*University of California, Irvine*

BEDFORD/ST. MARTIN'S     Boston   ♦   New York

*For Mimi*

**For Bedford/St. Martin's**

*Publisher for History:* Patricia A. Rossi
*Director of Development for History:* Jane Knetzger
*Developmental Editor:* Michael Weber
*Associate Editor, Publishing Services:* Maria Teresa Burwell
*Production Supervisor:* Jennifer Wetzel
*Senior Marketing Manager:* Jenna Bookin Barry
*Project Management:* Books By Design, Inc.
*Indexing:* Books By Design, Inc.
*Text Design:* Claire Seng-Niemoeller
*Photo Research:* Alice Lundoff
*Cover Design:* Billy Boardman
*Cover Photos: Hospital Scene,* Culver Pictures; *inset of Louisa May Alcott,*
    The Granger Collection
*Composition:* Stratford Publishing Services
*Printing and Binding:* Haddon Craftsmen, an RR Donnelley & Sons Company

*President:* Joan E. Feinberg
*Editorial Director:* Denise B. Wydra
*Director of Marketing:* Karen Melton Soeltz
*Director of Editing, Design, and Production:* Marcia Cohen
*Manager, Publishing Services:* Emily Berleth

Library of Congress Control Number: 2003103953

9  8  7  6  5  4
f  e  d  c  b  a

*For information, write:* Bedford/St. Martin's, 75 Arlington Street, Boston, MA 02116
(617-399-4000)

ISBN: 0-312-26028-8

# Foreword

The Bedford Series in History and Culture is designed so that readers can study the past as historians do.

The historian's first task is finding the evidence. Documents, letters, memoirs, interviews, pictures, movies, novels, or poems can provide facts and clues. Then the historian questions and compares the sources. There is more to do than in a courtroom, for hearsay evidence is welcome, and the historian is usually looking for answers beyond act and motive. Different views of an event may be as important as a single verdict. How a story is told may yield as much information as what it says.

Along the way the historian seeks help from other historians and perhaps from specialists in other disciplines. Finally, it is time to write, to decide on an interpretation and how to arrange the evidence for readers.

Each book in this series contains an important historical document or group of documents, each document a witness from the past and open to interpretation in different ways. The documents are combined with some element of historical narrative—an introduction or a biographical essay, for example—that provides students with an analysis of the primary source material and important background information about the world in which it was produced.

Each book in the series focuses on a specific topic within a specific historical period. Each provides a basis for lively thought and discussion about several aspects of the topic and the historian's role. Each is short enough (and inexpensive enough) to be a reasonable one-week assignment in a college course. Whether as classroom or personal reading, each book in the series provides firsthand experience of the challenge— and fun—of discovering, recreating, and interpreting the past.

Natalie Zemon Davis
Ernest R. May
Lynn Hunt
David W. Blight

# Preface

Louisa May Alcott's 1863 *Hospital Sketches* offers unparalleled insight into the world of Civil War America. An exceptionally engaging account of Alcott's stint as a nurse for wounded soldiers in Washington, D.C., during the winter of 1862–63, *Hospital Sketches* is written with all the humor and pathos Alcott is renowned for. It also has much to tell readers about women's lives during the Civil War; the experiences of wounded soldiers and the medical care they received; the profound links between home front and battlefront in wartime; changing attitudes toward race at the time of the Emancipation Proclamation; and popular war literature and its audiences.

As teachers of Civil War history know, the number of available materials that bring to life the social history of the war has increased enormously in recent years. Soldiers' diaries from both the Union and the Confederacy, as well as a multitude of Southern women's diaries, have given students a chance to understand the experience and underlying issues of the war through ordinary as well as extraordinary people's lives. Yet there are surprisingly few primary sources that explore Northern women's experiences of the war, whether on the home front or as nurses in hospitals.

Alcott's *Hospital Sketches* fills this important need. "I long to be a man," Alcott confided to her journal in April 1861 at the start of the war, "but as I can't fight, I will content myself with working for those who can." Eager to do her part for the war, in late 1862 Alcott volunteered as a Union nurse, becoming one of a pathbreaking group of women who transformed what had been an all-male profession before the war. She arrived at the Union Hotel Hospital in Georgetown at a dramatic moment—just after the horrific Union defeat at the Battle of Fredericksburg—and as a result she witnessed the shattering aftermath of battle, in which men "riddled with shot and shell," who had "borne suffering for which we have no name," were unloaded from crude carts at the hospital.[1] Alcott spent six weeks at the Union Hotel Hospital before succumbing to illness and returning home to Concord, Massachusetts.

Detailing her experiences in a lively collection of sketches first published in the *Commonwealth* magazine, Alcott reprinted them as a book in the summer of 1863. Readers of this vividly realized volume will not be surprised that *Hospital Sketches* was an immediate success upon publication, but Alcott was astonished and delighted. After years of struggle as a writer, Alcott achieved her first significant literary success, and she found the experience heady. Thus *Hospital Sketches* marked a significant turning point in a remarkable career that would produce not only adult novels such as *Moods* (1865) and *Work* (1872), but also the juvenile novels for which Alcott is best known, including *Little Women* (1868).

It is easy to see why Alcott's Northern audience responded favorably to her work. Within the pages of *Hospital Sketches,* Alcott brought to life the daily rhythms of a hospital during the Civil War with exceptional acuity. Civilians on the home front were avidly interested in the experiences of "our boys," as well as extremely curious about the brand-new phenomenon of women nurses, and Alcott provided a window into this new aspect of Civil War hospital life like no other observer. Among Civil War writers, only Walt Whitman had a comparable eye for the telling details of hospital life, but his *Speciman Days,* published after the war in 1872, did not reflect on the role of women in the war.

Many other observers of hospital life during the Civil War wrote accounts in high-flown, heroic, florid, and inevitably stiff and pretentious prose. In such writings, soldiers often emerged as superhuman beings who never complained or cried or even made noise within a hospital ward. In contrast, Alcott insisted on what she saw as the individual realities of these men, who emerged as unique, compelling characters. Some of Alcott's men did indeed cope in silence with their wounds and the terrible stresses of war, but others suffered mental breakdowns—what during World War I would be labeled shell shock. In admitting the terrible psychological as well as physical hardships imposed by war, Alcott was unique among her contemporaries.

Yet *Hospital Sketches* is not a "realistic" account, and some readers will find it of interest to analyze the work as a piece of literature and to think about what kind of Civil War Alcott was intent on creating

---

[1]*Hospital Sketches,* 70. Page numbers refer to this edition.

through the multiple devices of her prose. While Alcott explicitly eschewed romance, her text is nevertheless infused with nineteenth-century sentimentalism. In addition, Alcott was constantly torn between adherence to the strictures of sentimental domesticity for women and rebellion against their confining influence. For all readers, however, *Hospital Sketches* raises important questions about war and its meanings. How important are women's contributions to war? How do we justify the deaths of men in war? How do we justify war itself? These are questions that underlie Alcott's text, and they remain as fresh today as they were in Louisa May Alcott's time.

## FEATURES OF THIS EDITION

This edition of *Hospital Sketches* is unique in that it offers several features intended to make the work more accessible to students. A general introduction provides background, context, and analysis that I hope will aid students in addressing the issues raised in the work. First I discuss the Alcott family and Alcott's career prior to the writing of *Hospital Sketches,* her decision to become a nurse, and hospital life and medical care at the time of the Civil War. Next I consider the work's creation and reception. Then I take up Alcott's writing style and the literary influences upon it. Charles Dickens was the strongest influence, but in *Hospital Sketches* Alcott created her own lively style. Considerations of style lead directly to a discussion of what *Hospital Sketches* tells us about Alcott's and her era's ideas of gender and race, heroism, and the meaning of war. I point out, for example, that Alcott employed several techniques—such as using military metaphors (often humorously) and images of nurses as mothers and of soldiers as children—to express her views on the role of women in the war and in society generally. I also show how *Hospital Sketches* reveals that Alcott, like many Northern abolitionists, had complicated attitudes toward race. Finally, I place *Hospital Sketches* in its contemporary context as part of an outpouring of commercial war literature.

Glosses in the form of footnotes have been added to the text of *Hospital Sketches* to explain unusual terms, literary references, and the like. The text is followed by a detailed chronology of Alcott's life; questions for students to consider; and a selected bibliography of works on Alcott, nursing and medicine during the Civil War, women's history and the war, and the war itself. The volume concludes with an index. Also included in this edition are relevant illustrations from the period: two prints from *Harper's Weekly,* a photograph of Dorothea Dix, a painting of the Battle of Fredericksburg, and reproductions of two pages from the first edition of *Hospital Sketches.*

## A NOTE ON THE TEXT

The text reprinted here is taken from the 1863 edition of *Hospital Sketches,* published by James Redpath of Boston. No changes have been made to Alcott's text. Original spellings have been kept throughout. Alcott republished *Hospital Sketches* in 1869 with a few minor alterations. Since then, *Hospital Sketches* has rarely been out of print.

## ACKNOWLEDGMENTS

It is a pleasure to acknowledge the help I have received in editing *Hospital Sketches.* I am first of all grateful to David Blight for his suggestion that I contribute a book to the Bedford Series in History and Culture, and for his enthusiastic endorsement of this project from its inception. I am grateful as well to Patricia Rossi and Michael Weber for skillfully and patiently shepherding me through the editorial process at Bedford/St. Martin's. For their thoughtful readings and helpful suggestions, I am also grateful to Jean Baker of Goucher College, Kathleen Diffley of the University of Iowa, Lesley J. Gordon of the University of Akron, Patrick J. Kelly of the University of Texas–San Antonio, Lyde Cullen Sizer of Sarah Lawrence College, and Joan Waugh of the University of California, Los Angeles. Tracy Sachtjen provided helpful research assistance. I wish to thank Charlie Chubb, as always, for his support and encouragement. Finally, I dedicate this book to Mimi Chubb, whose acute editorial eye and skill as a writer never cease to amaze me.

Alice Fahs

# Contents

**APPENDIXES**

# Illustrations

THE BEDFORD SERIES IN HISTORY AND CULTURE

# Hospital Sketches
## by Louisa May Alcott

# PART ONE

# Introduction:
# Louisa May Alcott's
# Civil War

"I've often longed to see a war," Louisa May Alcott confided to her journal in April 1861, "and now I have my wish." Like so many other Americans at the start of the Civil War, Alcott was initially swept up in war fever in her hometown of Concord, Massachusetts. "The town is a high state of topsey turveyness," she wrote to a friend in May, "for every one is boiling over with excitement & when quiet Concord does get stirred up it is a sight to behold." Not only did "all the young men & boys drill with all their might," but the "women & girls sew & prepare for nurses," while the "old folks settle the fate of the Nation in groves of newspapers, & the children make the streets hideous with distracted drums & fifes." Signs of patriotism were everywhere: "Everyone wears cockades wherever one can be stuck, flags flap over head like parti colored birds of prey, patriotic balmorals,[1] cravats, handkerchiefs & hats are all the rig, & if we keep on at our present rate everything in heaven & earth will soon be confined to red, white, & blue, & 'Hail Columbia' take the place of our Yankee 'How are yer?' "[2]

As even this brief, informal sketch in a letter to a friend revealed, in 1861 Alcott was already an accomplished writer adept at rapidly conjuring up a lively scene in vital, humorous prose. Yet at the start of the Civil War, the soon-to-be-famous author of *Little Women* (1868) was only at the beginning of her publishing career, with just a few short stories, poems, and a slender volume of "fairy stories," *Flower Fables,*

1

to her credit—and years of frustration as a writer behind her. Her 1863 *Hospital Sketches,* a fictionalized account of her brief experiences as a nurse in Washington, was a gratifying and unexpected publishing success that marked a major turning point in her writing career. It is also a Civil War classic, a book in which Alcott brought to bear all the qualities of her vivid, Dickensian prose on her wartime experiences, providing us with rich insights into women's lives in mid-nineteenth-century America, their wartime roles, the often shocking medical conditions of wartime hospitals for wounded soldiers, the experiences of common soldiers themselves, and racial prejudice at the time of the Civil War. Part of a vast outpouring of popular Civil War literature published during the war itself, *Hospital Sketches* also has much to teach us about mid-nineteenth-century literary culture and the ways in which war was imagined for a Northern reading public. Offering a moving combination of humor and pathos, *Hospital Sketches* provides unparalleled insight into the world of Civil War America.[3]

## THE ALCOTT FAMILY

Louisa May Alcott, born in 1832 and twenty-eight years old when war broke out in April 1861, was part of a close-knit family within the remarkable literary community of Concord, Massachusetts. Readers of the 1868 *Little Women* will remember the four fictional March daughters, Meg, Jo, Beth, and Amy, who lived at home during the Civil War with their mother, Marmee, while their father served as a soldier. The fictional March sisters were in fact closely modeled on the four Alcott sisters, Anna, Louisa, Elizabeth, and Abby May; Louisa even occasionally referred to herself as Jo in her later journals. The character of Marmee, too, was closely modeled on Louisa's mother, Abba, whom she revered. But in contrast to Jo March in the novel, Louisa at the time of the war lived alone at home with her parents. Her beloved oldest sister, Anna, Louisa's "one bosom friend and comforter," had married in 1860; her younger sister Elizabeth, a "dear little shadow," "so sweet and patient and so worn," had died at home in 1858, several years after contracting scarlet fever; and her youngest sister, Abby May, to whom Louisa was not close and somewhat jealously characterized as "one of the fortunate ones" who "gets what she wants easily," spent much of 1861 teaching art and music in Syracuse, New York.[4]

Far from her father having been absent as a soldier during the war, as in *Little Women,* he was a superintendent of local schools in Concord. A good friend of Ralph Waldo Emerson and a minor figure among the Transcendentalists (antebellum idealists who believed in a radical, transcendent individualism), Bronson Alcott was a philosopher and reformer who engaged in numerous reform and educational projects throughout his life. With his wife and children, he had briefly participated in a utopian experiment in communal living at Fruitlands, a farm in Massachusetts, in 1843. That experiment had failed in large part due to Alcott's dreamy impracticality; indeed, for his wife and children, Fruitlands had been an ordeal in which they ate only fruits and nuts and in which Abba carried the load of all household work. Bronson Alcott also founded several experimental schools throughout his life, and on the eve of the Civil War, he received the appointment as superintendent of schools.[5]

Deeply interested in education throughout his life, Bronson took an especially active role in his daughters' schooling, requiring that they keep self-scrutinizing journals as children, for example. Yet although Bronson Alcott was energetically involved in his daughters' lives, it is telling that in *Little Women* Louisa portrayed the March sisters' father as absent, for that portrait captured a certain reality of Bronson Alcott's life: his "absence" from the expected middle-class role of breadwinner and provider for his family. It was a role Alcott found difficult, even impossible, to fulfill, and this inability had a profound impact on his family. Bronson Alcott, however beloved a figure of philosophy, was both deeply impractical and inept at making money, and thus the Alcott family constantly struggled to make ends meet.

His failure as a lecturer was a case in point. Like many of his contemporaries, including Emerson, Bronson Alcott was interested in lecturing as a mode of reaching a wider public. Lecturing was in fact a potentially lucrative practice in the mid-nineteenth century, both a form of popular entertainment and a mode of disseminating knowledge. Many of the most popular lecturers of the day could make substantial sums as they toured the country; Emerson himself had great success in making lecture tours of the "West" (the Midwest). But Alcott was unable to make money as a lecturer, as Louisa's journals poignantly recorded.

In 1853, with a gift of $18 from Emerson, Bronson Alcott set out on a lecture tour of the "West." While he was gone, his wife was forced to take in boarders to make ends meet, and clearly the family pinned their financial hopes on Bronson's endeavor. Louisa described the "dramatic scene when he arrived" home late at night in February

1854. The "half-frozen wanderer" was "hungry, tired, cold, and disappointed, but smiling bravely and as serene as ever." The family "fed and warmed and brooded over him, longing to ask if he had made any money, but no one did till little May said, after he had told all the pleasant things, 'Well, did people pay you?' Then, with a queer look, he opened his pocket-book and showed one dollar, saying with a smile that made our eyes fill, 'Only that! My overcoat was stolen, and I had to buy a shawl. Many promises were not kept, and travelling is costly; but I have opened the way, and another year shall do better.'"[6]

But Bronson Alcott did not do better another year. On the eve of war, as the "sage of Concord," he offered philosophical "conversations" to select audiences in addition to acting as superintendent. But these "conversations" did not earn him much money, although friends helped out as best they could by supporting him with surreptitious acts of charity. As Louisa noted in 1861, "Father had four talks at Emerson's; good people came, and he enjoyed them much; made $30. R. W. E. [Emerson] probably put in $20. He has a sweet way of bestowing gifts on the table under a book or behind a candle-stick, when he thinks Father wants a little money, and no one will help him earn. A true friend is this tender and illustrious man." But clearly such gifts could only go so far.[7]

## THE STRUGGLE FOR WORK

The truth was that in the years leading up to the Civil War, the Alcott family faced a constant hard grind that weighed heavily in particular on Louisa. "How poor we are," Louisa confided to her journal in 1850 at age seventeen, and "how much worry it is to live." From an early age, Louisa shouldered the burden of adding to her family's income, sometimes as its sole breadwinner. "Poor as rats & apparently quite forgotten by every one but the Lord," she wrote at age nineteen in 1851, a year during which she recorded earning $40 as a governess, $40 for her sewing, $10 for selling a story to a popular literary magazine, and $4 as a servant—the last a bitter experience she gave up after a month of being "starved & frozen." Two years later, economic necessity again drove Alcott to be a "second girl," or servant; she earned $2 a week in 1853 during a summer of work that included doing the wash for another family. That summer was "distasteful and lonely," she recorded in her journal. In 1858, she recorded that she had gone to Boston on her "usual hunt for employment," as she seemed "to be the only bread-winner just now."[8]

For all their continuing economic trials, the Alcott family was in fact relatively privileged in comparison to most working-class and immigrant men and women, as well as free blacks, who had many fewer resources to draw on and few choices in work. Louisa was a part-time, not a full-time, servant; she never worked in a factory; and she could engage in such "genteel" work as teaching. In addition, Abba Alcott received an inheritance that allowed the family to buy a house in Concord, providing them with the stability they much needed after moving frequently during Louisa's childhood. Though the Alcott family constantly scrambled for money, many families faced a different, more drastic kind of poverty, and some of these families were in fact the objects of the Alcotts' charity. In 1852, while the family was briefly living in Boston, Louisa recorded that her mother had engaged in "city missionary work," a form of "practical Christianity" in which Abba attempted to help poor girls find places as servants. Their own "poor little home" had become a "shelter for lost girls, abused wives, friendless children, and weak or wicked men." Although her parents had "no money to give," they gave their "time, sympathy," and "help." If "blessings would make them rich, they would be millionaires," Louisa noted. Such charity work continued in the years leading up to the Civil War, and in an incident to be memorialized in *Little Women,* Louisa's 1856 journal recorded that her sister Elizabeth had fallen "very ill with scarlet-fever caught from some poor children Mother nursed when they fell sick, living over a cellar where pigs had been kept." The landlord, she noted, "would not clean the place till Mother threatened to sue him for allowing a nuisance."[9]

Yet though the Alcotts never faced dire poverty, their hold on middle-class status was nevertheless precarious. The struggle to make money was always on Louisa's mind, as her journals and letters make dramatically clear: not only do they carefully record her earnings, but they record her constant frustrations with such tasks as endlessly mending old clothes. She did not try to hide her poverty: in 1862, when she met the author Rebecca Harding Davis in Boston at a reception, she told Davis that she had had to travel home to Concord that day to bring back a gown, because it was "the only decent one" she had. "I'm very poor," she announced and, according to Davis, in the "next breath" told her that she had "once taken a place as 'second girl.'" Davis remembered her as a "tall, thin young woman," who was "plainly dressed, and had that watchful, defiant air with which the woman whose youth is slipping away is apt to face the world which has offered no place to her." Alcott was twenty-nine at the time.[10]

The constant search for work was a major theme of Alcott's journals before the Civil War. But there were few choices for middle-class women in an era that celebrated women's "domesticity" and the new ideology of "separate spheres," counseling them in magazines such as *Godey's Lady's Book* to stay at home and make a "haven in a heartless world" while their husbands engaged in business. Teaching was a respectable occupation, but as Louisa noted baldly in her journal in 1862, "Don't like to teach." Nevertheless, by that year Alcott—the daughter of an educational reformer, after all—had taught school numerous times, often in her own home. In 1853, she started a "little school" of local children that met in her parlor. It was "a hard year," she concluded, "tiresome with school and people I didn't like." In 1854, she taught in a school established by her father, which Bronson Alcott cheerfully called "a pleasant one of some dozen or fourteen little children, and the profits to all worth naming, they, the teachers getting good experiences." But the father's sanguine view was not shared by his daughter. "School for me month after month" is all she bleakly recorded of this "pleasant" experience. She continued teaching periodically in the years leading up to the Civil War, and in 1862, when she received an offer during the war to help her start a school, she accepted, noting that she had to "take what comes." But she found it "distasteful work" and left it behind as soon as she could. As she noted in 1859, "won't teach any more if I can help it; don't like it; and if I can get writing enough can do much better."[11]

Sewing was another common way for women to earn money, but it was a difficult mode of making a living. In the mid-nineteenth century, the genteel "starving seamstress" was a literary figure that populated numerous popular stories, and it had some basis in fact. Women who attempted to support themselves through sewing were usually paid by the piece, and rarely did such pay provide a living wage. Alcott herself provided dramatic proof of this fact: as she noted in 1856, "sewed a great deal, and got very tired; one job for Mr. G. of a dozen pillow-cases, one dozen sheets, six fine cambric neckties, and two dozen handkerchiefs, at which I had to work all one night to get them done, as they were a gift to him. I got only $4."[12]

Alcott did not attempt to support herself through sewing alone; but numerous women, particularly in large cities, did attempt to earn their keep solely through needlework. Their situation only worsened during the Civil War, as the prices they received for their work from army contractors were driven down by middlemen. Indeed, it was the Civil War that "provided the background against which wage-earning women began to re-evaluate their condition," historian Alice Kessler-

Harris has noted. In November 1863, a number of sewing women in New York founded the Working Women's Union, and some three hundred of them met "to bring the subject of the miserable pay received by them before the public." Their protests gained the sympathetic attention of several writers, including the famously tart-tongued *New York Ledger* columnist Fanny Fern (Sara Parton), but did little to improve their condition. Later, Alcott herself would consider the plight of such working women in her 1873 novel *Work*.[13]

As Alcott realistically noted, "sewing won't make my fortune." Yet over and over Alcott recorded sewing to make clothing for her family and to make some money, often "sewing in the evening when my day's work was done," as she wrote in 1854. Such work revealed the limited range of options open to women who needed to make money. It was not work she loved.[14]

*That* work, of course, was writing. Indeed, the pleasure Alcott took in writing was a running refrain throughout her journals and letters. "I am in the garret with my papers round me," she noted with satisfaction in April 1855, "and a pile of apples to eat while I write my journal, plan stories, and enjoy the patter of rain on the roof, in peace and quiet." Writing was constantly on her mind; over and over again she noted that stories were "simmering" away as she did chores: "I can simmer novels while I do my housework," she said in August 1858, "so see my way to a little money, and perhaps more by-and-by if I ever make a hit." Writing was clearly a dramatic outlet for her within the constricted life she led: "Worked off my stage fever in writing a story, and felt better," she noted in one journal entry.[15]

Alcott's journals and letters show that she yearned for recognition and fame as a writer. In 1855, she noted proudly that "the principal event of the winter is the appearance of my book 'Flower Fables'" (her collection of fairy tales). She was delighted that it "sold very well" and reported that "people began to think that topsey-turvey Louisa would amount to something after all." Two years later, she wondered after reading a biography of Charlotte Brontë "if I shall ever be famous enough for people to care to read my story and struggles." In 1858, she wrote that "I hope I shall yet do my great book, for that seems to be my work, and I am growing up to it. I even think of trying the 'Atlantic' [the most prominent literary journal of the day]. There's ambition for you!" When one of her stories was in fact accepted by the *Atlantic Monthly* in 1859, she told herself that she had "not been pegging away all these years in vain, and may yet have books and publishers and a fortune of my own." Ambition was a keynote of her literary career, but it was hard for any woman in mid-nineteenth-century America to reconcile literary ambition with the conventional assumption that women would remain in the home as private, not public, figures.[16]

## ALCOTT'S EARLY LITERARY CAREER

For a young would-be writer, Louisa May Alcott was extraordinarily well connected within the remarkable literary community of Concord. Among the Alcotts' closest friends and neighbors was Ralph Waldo Emerson, and they saw Henry David Thoreau frequently as well. When Thoreau died in May 1862, Bronson Alcott read selections from Thoreau's works at his funeral, and Louisa described the "lovely day clear, & calm, & spring like," on which she and her fellow townsmen "walked after Henry's coffin with its fall of flowers." The Alcotts were also acquainted with Nathaniel Hawthorne, although the two families were not close; in a typically humorous mode, Louisa wrote that she sometimes caught "glimpses" of the "dark mysterious" Hawthorne "skimming by as if he expected the house of Alcott were about to rush out and clutch him."[17]

Farther afield in Boston (about twenty miles from Concord), the Alcotts had additional prominent literary friends and acquaintances, including James T. Fields, editor of the elite literary journal the *Atlantic Monthly* and publisher of Ticknor and Fields, the most prestigious book publishing firm of the mid-nineteenth century. Louisa sometimes stayed at the Fields's home, a center of Boston literary life. As she commented in April 1862, she had "visited about at J. T. Fields the great publishers where I saw Mrs. Stowe, Fanny Kemble, Holmes, Longfellow, & all the fine folks besides living in style in a very smart house with very clever people who have filled it with books, pictures, statues & beautiful things picked up on their travels." Alcott was also acquainted with the abolitionist and author James Redpath, who would become her publisher during the war; and with Moncure Conway, the editor of the radical abolitionist newspaper the *Commonwealth*.[18]

Louisa May Alcott may have known some of the most eminent literary figures of her day, but on the eve of the Civil War, these connections had certainly not translated into the literary success she yearned for. True, she had published a number of stories in "story papers," cheap periodicals printed in newspaper format and selling for a nickel or dime, but these she had published anonymously. In addition, the prestigious *Atlantic Monthly,* edited before the war by the famous writer James Russell Lowell, had published her story "Love and Self-Love" in March 1860 and then her story "A Modern Cinderella; Or, The Little Old Shoe," in October 1860 and had accepted another of her stories, "Debby's Début," by the end of that year. Yet at some point the magazine's new editor, James T. Fields, who took over the magazine shortly after the outbreak of war, apparently told her, "Stick to your teaching; you can't write," a piece of advice that rankled for years. "I won't teach; and I can write, and I'll prove it," she recorded herself defiantly answering. Fields's advice was patronizing and misguided, but he no doubt meant well according to his own lights. He knew, as did all the Alcotts' friends, how desperately poor the family was and that teaching was steadier work than writing.[19]

Financial need, coupled with the grinding work she was forced to do—what she called "hard grubbing"—shaped her early literary career in several ways. First, her writing was constantly interrupted because she had to sew, or clean, or take care of her father or mother (or other relatives) when they were sick. If teaching and other forms of paid work were an interruption from her beloved writing, so too was the endless housework she engaged in. At the same time, because she needed to earn money from her writing, an occasional publication in an elite journal like the *Atlantic Monthly* could not possibly suffice for her needs. "Money is my end & aim just now," she commented in the summer of 1861, and as a result she found the "slow coach" *Atlantic* extremely frustrating because it was so desultory about both publication and payment. In August 1861, she was still waiting for her story "Debby's Début" to appear, though the magazine had had it "most a year." (It finally appeared in August 1863.) As she commented, "I don't care two straws if old 'Debby' never makes her 'Début' except that I cant send another till she is well out of the way." Reflecting the reading public's absorption in the war at the beginning of the conflict, James T. Fields told her he had to choose "war stories if he can, to suit the times"; Alcott commented to a friend that she would write " 'great guns' Hail Columbia & Concord fight, if he'll only take it for money is the staff of life & without one falls flat no matter how much genius he may carry."[20]

To earn money, throughout the war Alcott continued to publish a number of what she called "blood & thunder " stories in popular weekly magazines (the so-called story papers) such as *Frank Leslie's Illustrated*

*Newspaper.* These sensational stories, part of a larger popular melodra-matic literature in mid-nineteenth-century America, emphasized bold action, sharply drawn heroes and villains, striking effects on the emo-tions, and lurid, exciting plots. Alcott clearly took pleasure in writing these stories, which one critic has called her "female revenge thrill-ers." They apparently acted as a form of emotional release. Late in the war, she commented in her journal that she had written "a blood & thunder story or novelette of several hundred pages to relieve my feel-ings." Expatiating at more length elsewhere in her journal, she wrote, "I enjoy romancing to suit myself; and though my tales are silly, they are not bad; and my sinners always have a good spot somewhere." Besides, she reported, "Mr. L. [Frank Leslie] says my tales are so 'dra-matic, vivid, and full of plot,' they are just what he wants."[21]

Most importantly, of course, these stories earned good money: "Wrote 'King of Clubs,'—$30," she noted in April 1862 with satisfac-tion, commenting that the story "made more than all my months of teaching." For "Pauline's Passion and Punishment," which won a prize from *Leslie's,* she received $100 in 1862. By contrast, for her six weeks of nursing soldiers she was to earn only $10. Alcott was proud that her stories earned money for her family, but she was also aware that in the literary hierarchy of the day such popular stories ranked far below the status of stories published in the *Atlantic Monthly.* Tellingly, she published her *Frank Leslie's* stories anonymously. Her internal con-flicts about this kind of literature would be played out in the plot of *Little Women,* in which Jo March had the task of learning to write "from the heart" instead of producing the kinds of sensational potboil-ers that in fact helped Alcott support her family.[22]

## THE COMING OF WAR

The outbreak of war transformed life in Concord. As in small towns all over the North, young men formed local companies and excitedly began to drill as soldiers. For example, Edward Waldo Emerson, the son of Ralph Waldo Emerson, formed the "Concord Cadets," and Alcott recorded their doings with amusement as she watched them "poke each others eyes out, bang their heads & blow themselves up with gunpowder most valiantly." They "will do good service by & by I've no doubt if there is anything left of them when ordered to the field," she concluded with dry humor.[23]

Over the course of the war, Alcott would report on the "Concord Company" in a number of letters, revealing just how tight was the link between home front and battlefront for most Americans, and how local the contest. After the Union defeat at Bull Run in July 1861, for instance, Alcott wrote of five Concord men "missing either killed or captured," including "Cyrus Hosmer & Sydney Rice," whom she knew personally. A year later, she recorded the return of "our boys" after "a years imprisonment in various places," telling her correspondent that "they were taken at Bulls Run, you know." "Of course the town got up a row," she said, "banged drums, fired cannon, tooted & bawled, gave banners to the breeze, dinners eaten, odes sung, speeches made & a grand hurrah-boys generally." But by this time, she was somewhat cynical about the returning "boys," characterizing them as some of the Union soldiers who had run away during battle. "'Our gallant fellow citizens' who ran away & very justly got caught, look fat, brown, & lazy, & loaf about making a large spittoon of the Mill-Dam as they spin yarns & condecendingly regard their friends as if the nation was under everlasting obligations to them & all should fall down & adore."[24]

If she was somewhat skeptical about the "heroism" of her townsmen after the rout of Union troops at Bull Run, she felt differently in the fall of 1863, when other members of "our Concord company" returned, seasoned by the war. She recorded the excitement of the town, which was "in as wild a state of excitement as it is possible for such a dozy old place to be without dying of brain fever." "Flags are flapping every where, wreaths & 'Welcome home' are stuck on every stickable place & our drum corps, consisting of eight small boys with eight large drums, keep a continual rub-a-dubbing," she reported.[25]

In a society whose gender arrangements did not allow women to be soldiers, Alcott felt envious of the men who went off to war. "I long to be a man," she wrote in her journal, "but as I can't fight, I will content myself with working for those who can." Indeed, when war broke out Alcott, like many other Northern women, immediately began to labor as part of a home-front war effort of female production, "sewing violently on patriotic blue shirts," as she humorously put it in a May 1861 letter. In the early months of war, many commentators stressed the importance of women's war work in sewing uniforms and havelocks (cloth pieces to attach to caps to protect soldiers from the sun), preparing and packing provisions, or knitting socks and mittens for the volunteer and initially underprovisioned army. The most popular

# HARPER'S WEEKLY
## A JOURNAL OF CIVILIZATION.

VOL. V.—No. 235.]      NEW YORK, SATURDAY, JUNE 29, 1861.      [ SINGLE COPIES SIX CENTS. $2.00 PER YEAR IN ADVANCE.

Entered according to Act of Congress, in the Year 1861, by Harper & Brothers, in the Clerk's Office of the District Court for the Southern District of New York.

THE WAR—MAKING HAVELOCKS FOR THE VOLUNTEERS.

This 1861 illustration shows Northern women making havelocks—a flap attached to a cap to protect the neck against the sun or bad weather—for Union Army volunteers.

New-York Historical Society

magazine of the day, *Harper's Weekly,* printed a propagandistic cover illustration of women industriously sewing "havelocks for the volunteers." Numerous other magazines and papers also carried stories, illustrations, and poems extolling women's war work. In the early months of war, women's production was necessary to what was at first a decidedly amateur war.[26]

But while sewing was one of the prescribed activities a woman could contribute to the war effort, it was never a particularly satisfying endeavor for Alcott. "I lay down my needle & take up my pen with great inward contentment," she wrote to a friend, "the first article being my abomination & the last my delight." Yet if anything the war meant that Alcott had more sewing to do and even less time to write: "Stories simmered in my brain, demanding to be writ, but I let them simmer," she wrote in her journal. May Day 1861 found her with "three hundred women all sewing together at the hall for two days." At the same time, she continued to do substantial amounts of family sewing, noting that in April she "sewed a good deal" getting her sister May's "things in order, as she sent for me to make and mend and buy and send her outfit." Sewing was work she despised but could not seem to get away from.[27]

She yearned instead for a more active role in the war. "If I was only a boy I'd march off tomorrow," she wrote in early 1862, in what was for her a reiterated theme throughout the war. Since she could not become a soldier (although some women did in fact disguise themselves as men in order to enlist), she sought other means "to help if I can." In 1862, she thought about going to Port Royal, South Carolina, which had come under Union control early in the war, in order to teach the "contrabands," or newly freed slaves. Indeed, she noted that she had been "chosen to go from Concord before the word came that unmarried women were forbidden." She chafed under such gender restrictions: "I offered to go as teacher on one of the Islands but Mr. Philbrey objected because I had no natural protector to go with me, so I was obliged to give that up," she informed one correspondent in late 1863. She also heard that there was "to be a school in Washington for the blacks" and commented that "if I am asked I shall go as I like the plan."[28]

Alcott's interest in work with newly freed slaves was consonant with her family's long-held antislavery sentiments. As early as age ten, Alcott had recorded in her journal a visit to her family from the antislavery activist Parker Pillsbury, noting that "we talked about the poor slaves." In 1859, she wrote of John Brown's famous raid at Harpers

Ferry, a failed attempt to incite a slave insurrection, as a "heroic act." After Brown's execution in December, she attended a public meeting in Concord at which Emerson, Thoreau, and her father spoke with "reverence and admiration for the martyr." Alcott herself contributed an ode on Brown's death, "With a Rose, That Bloomed on the Day of John Brown's Martyrdom," in which she wrote:

> And the gallows only proved to him
> A stepping-stone to heaven.

It was first published in the antislavery journal the *Liberator* before being reprinted in James Redpath's testimonial volume, *Echoes of Harper's Ferry.* Two of John Brown's daughters later briefly boarded with the Alcotts.[29]

Alcott continued to hope she could find a way to aid the newly freed slaves throughout the war: "I should like of all things to go South & help the blacks," she wrote in late 1863, and in the wake of her success with *Hospital Sketches,* she was delighted that James T. Fields "wanted the letters I should write" if she were able to go "to Port Royal to teach contrabands." But apparently, Alcott could find no way to travel south as a single woman and was forced to find other means by which to aid the cause of black freedom. In July 1863, she noted that she had "made an article of some letters from Miss Swetts colored pupils at Readville, for the Commonwealth." And in November 1863, she recorded sewing for the Union cause, but this time for a black regiment: "Sewed for Wheeler's colored company & sent them comfort-bags, towels, books, & bed sacks," she noted. Her pride in the revolutionary creation of black regiments was evident in her brief year-end summary for 1863: "The first colored regiment went to the war," she noted. At the end of *Hospital Sketches,* she commented that "the next hospital I enter will, I hope, be one for the colored regiments."[30]

## BECOMING A NURSE

But ultimately, it was as a Union nurse, not as a teacher of freedmen and freedwomen, that Alcott found a way to contribute more actively to the war effort. As early as May 1861, Alcott had begun to think about becoming a nurse, asking her friend Alfred Whitman, "Are you going to have a dab at the saucy Southerners? I long to fly at some body & free my mind on several points, but there is no opening for me at present so I study Dr. Home on 'Gun shot wounds,' & get my highly connected self ready to go as a nurse when the slow coaches at Washington begin to lay about them & get their fellow men into a comfortably smashed condition."[31]

In seeking to nurse wounded soldiers, Alcott was part of a pioneering group of women who entered and helped to transform the field of nursing during the war, in part inspired by the famous work of Florence Nightingale in the Crimea (1854). Nightingale's efforts to reform the unsanitary conditions of medical care within the British army had received wide attention in America through the publication of her *Notes on Hospitals* (1859) and *Notes on Nursing* (1860). So much a part of popular consciousness did she become that Henry Wadsworth Longfellow eulogized her as "A Lady with a Lamp," a "noble type of good / heroic womanhood," in his much-quoted 1857 *Atlantic Monthly* poem "Santa Filomena."[32]

On the eve of the Civil War in America, however, there were no female nurses attached to the Army; instead, male soldiers convalescing from illness typically acted as nurses. Women did have private experience with nursing, as doctors treated patients primarily at home and women were expected by tradition to help there with the care of their sick relatives. Some women also had experience working as "ward matrons" in hospitals associated with almshouses. There, they supervised patients' diets, as prescribed by a doctor, and were in charge of keeping a ward of about forty beds clean. Because of this experience, at the start of the war some women were offered positions as hospital ward matrons by army authorities in both the North and South. Hospitals, however, were primarily for the care of poor patients, not the general population.

At the start of the war, there were no nurses' training programs in existence; nor was there even a generally accepted understanding of who could claim to be a "nurse." Indeed, throughout the war a variety of men and women called themselves nurses, including occasional and regular hospital visitors, unpaid volunteers, matrons, convalescing soldiers, and members of large voluntary organizations such as the U.S. Sanitary Commission or the Christian Commission. The Civil War would act as a major professionalizing impulse for the field of nursing, but at the start of the war, there was little common understanding of who might be considered a nurse—or even exactly what a nurse's duties were.

A *Harper's Weekly* illustration during the Civil War paying tribute to the women nurses of the U.S. Sanitary Commission.

New-York Historical Society

Numerous Northern women were eager to volunteer to care for sick and wounded soldiers from the start of the war. As Alcott noted, "the height of my ambition was to go to the front after a battle." But they faced a number of obstacles, including initial resistance by the tradition-bound Army Medical Bureau to the very idea of female nurses. Still, within two weeks after the start of war, several women leaders had begun initiatives to allow women nurses to contribute to the war effort. In Washington, the well-known prison reformer Dorothea Dix lobbied for the creation of an Army Nursing Corps and was appointed superintendent of female nurses by the secretary of war. Dix was given unofficial authority to recruit army nurses, but without strong support from the surgeon general's office she never succeeded in putting into place a clear, logical system of nurse recruitment and employment. In New York, Dr. Elizabeth Blackwell called a meeting to discuss the training of nurses, which inspired additional meetings leading to the creation of the Women's Central Association of Relief (WCAR).[33]

The WCAR itself became an important arm of the U.S. Sanitary Commission, a powerful civilian organization that worked to create sanitary conditions for soldiers in hospitals and camps. Early in the war, the "Sanitary," as it was called, staffed hospital ships for the army with a number of female nurses. They were deemed so effective that in July 1862, the new surgeon general of the army, William Hammond, intent on reforming the antiquated army medical establishment, issued an order requiring that at least one-third of army nurses in general hospitals be women. The nuns of the Catholic Sisters of Charity were also an important source of female nurses. Because of their religious vows, there was little public resistance to their care of strange men's bodies, considered by many a shocking violation of propriety for other women at the start of the war.

Ultimately, more than three thousand Northern women served as army nurses in the war, including Louisa May Alcott. But many more women were involved in hospital work in both the North and South, whether they were officially designated nurses or not. According to Jane E. Schultz, over twenty thousand women worked as matrons, cooks, laundresses—and nurses—in Confederate and Union hospitals during the war. Many of these women were working-class white women or African American women; although they performed a variety of nursing tasks, the title "nurse" was more often given to middle-class white women like Alcott.[34]

Somewhat less is known about Confederate than Union female nurses, in part because of the burning of records during the fall of Richmond at the end of the war and also because Confederate hospitals failed systematically to record women's services. Still, numerous elite white Southern women volunteered to become nurses at the beginning of the war, and several, including Sally Louisa Tompkins and Juliet Opie Hopkins, set up private hospitals for the care of wounded soldiers. Slave women performed most of the domestic labor in Confederate hospitals. Recognizing women's contributions to the war effort, the Confederate Congress officially authorized women to become hospital nurses in September 1862. In the South, as in the North, resistance to women as nurses lessened as women proved themselves on the job and as the great need for their services became clear in an increasingly brutal war.

While Alcott knew early in the war that she would like to serve the Union through nursing, it took time for her to find a position as nurse. In October 1861, she was still "sewing and knitting for 'our boys' all the time." As the Union Army under the cautious General George McClellan delayed engaging the enemy week after week, she commented acerbically that "it seems as if a few energetic women could carry on the war better than the men do it so far." During November and December 1861, she noted that she "wrote, read, sewed, and wanted something to do." The next year offered more of the same: "Sewing Bees and Lint Picks [lint was used to make bandages] for 'our boys'" kept her busy during September and October of 1862. The horrific battles of that fall, including the costly Union victory at Antietam in September, created "anxious faces" and "beating hearts" in Concord but only increased Alcott's desire to participate in a more meaningful way in the war: "I like the stir in the air," she commented, "and long for battle like a warhorse when he smells powder."[35]

She finally found her opportunity in the winter of 1862. Through the help of an influential Boston acquaintance, Hannah Stevenson, who had served as a hospital nurse for over a year, she managed to get approval from Dorothea Dix to report to Washington as an army nurse. Dix was by all accounts neither an easy personality nor a gifted manager, though dedicated and well meaning. Worried about the reception of women nurses in Washington, she issued stern guidelines stating that "no woman under thirty need apply to serve in government hospitals. All nurses are required to be plain looking women. Their dresses must be brown or black, with no bows, no curls, no jewelry, and no hoops." Numerous young women chafed under what

Dorothea Dix, the "Superintendent of Female Nurses" in the North during the Civil War. Dix gave Alcott approval to serve as a nurse in Washington, D.C.

New York Public Library Picture Collection

Alcott called a "prunes-and-prisms doctrine," which discouraged their contributions to the war effort. Alcott herself was ambivalent about Dix. Once acquainted in Washington, Alcott called her a "kind soul but very queer & arbitrary," commenting that "no one likes her & I don't wonder." Tellingly, Alcott would "respectfully" dedicate *Hospital Sketches* not to Dix, but to her mentor Stevenson.[36]

Alcott, who turned thirty on November 29, 1862, explained in her journal why she had "decided to go to Washington as a nurse": "Help needed, and I love nursing, and *must* let out my pent-up energy in some new way." While worried about leaving her family, she also rationalized her departure: There would be "one less to feed and warm and worry over" with her gone, she decided. It was only at the last moment that she realized "I had taken my life in my hand, and might never see them all again." Imagining herself as a soldier going into battle, she envisioned her possible death—and did almost die of typhoid fever or pneumonia (it is not clear which was her diagnosis).[37]

Alcott was initially assigned to the Armory Square Hospital in Washington, a new hospital that had an excellent reputation as a well-run institution. Alcott later visited the Armory during her stay in Washington and praised its "neatness, comfort, and convenience," all of which aroused the "covetous propensities of such nurses as came from other hospitals to visit it." But at the last moment, she was reassigned to the Union Hotel Hospital in Georgetown, where "disorder, discomfort" and "bad management" held sway. The Union Hotel Hospital, which had indeed once been a hotel, had been hastily converted for use as a hospital in wartime—so hastily that some of its rooms, as Alcott tells us, still bore their old names, including "ballroom," on their doors. Because there were few hospitals in existence at the start of the war, a number of buildings, including taverns, hotels, factories, warehouses, and even prisons, were used as hospitals before a sizable program of building new hospitals began. (The Union Hotel Hospital is shown on the cover of this book.) Reporting to this "Hurly-burly House," as she called it, on December 14, 1862, Alcott arrived just before the wounded were brought in from one of the major battles of the war.[38]

## THE BATTLE OF FREDERICKSBURG

The disastrous December 13 Union defeat at Fredericksburg, which Alcott called the "Burnside blunder" (of Major General Ambrose Burnside) in *Hospital Sketches,* resulted in nearly 13,000 Union casualties, compared to around 5,000 for the Confederates.

Fredericksburg marked the end of an autumn of unprecedented slaughter. In the first year of the war, there had been few major battles, and President Lincoln had grown increasingly impatient with the cautious approach of his commander in chief, General George B. McClellan. In the west, Ulysses S. Grant emerged as a commander who could deliver victory, but in the east, McClellan hesitated to push "on to Richmond," the Confederate capital, as the newspapers kept urging. McClellan instead used much of 1861 and early 1862 to build up the Army of the Potomac into a powerful fighting force, but once he had achieved this goal, he was still reluctant to engage in battle. The so-called Peninsula Campaign during the spring of 1862 was his agonizingly slow attempt to move on Richmond; that campaign failed when McClellan withdrew instead of taking advantage of his superiority in force to rout the Confederate army.

Lincoln cajoled, pleaded, and persuaded. Finally, responding to General Robert E. Lee's first invasion of the North at Antietam, Maryland, on September 17, 1862, McClellan delivered the Union victory Lincoln needed to be able to proclaim his Preliminary Emancipation Proclamation of September 22. But it was the costliest single day of the war, with immense casualties of over 26,000 (around 13,000 Union troops), and what's more, McClellan failed once again to follow through by pursuing Lee's army back into Virginia. This failure was a major factor in Lincoln's decision to relieve McClellan as commander of the Army of the Potomac, appointing General Ambrose Burnside in his place on November 7.

But if Lincoln had hoped this change in command would result in victory, he did not get his wish. Burnside initiated a new campaign against Richmond in late 1862, and the result was the stunning defeat at Fredericksburg. There, wave after wave of Union troops were sent across open ground to be mowed down by Confederate soldiers who were well positioned on high ground. The battle involved some 100,000 Union and 72,000 Confederate soldiers and resulted in close to 18,000 killed, wounded, and missing.[39]

The slaughter at Fredericksburg was horrific. One soldier remembered that after the battle, "the field was covered all over with wounded men groaning and calling for water; some attempted to crawl on their bellies to the river side for a drop of water to relieve their thirst." All "suffered terribly from the cold," as they "had no way to warm" themselves.[40]

We get a striking glimpse of the aftermath of that battle in *Hospital Sketches*. Alcott describes the "stretchers, each with its legless, armless, or desperately wounded occupant" entering her ward, while more

The Battle of Fredericksburg, December 1862, as depicted in a contemporary painting.
New York Public Library Picture Collection

able-bodied men were "ragged, gaunt and pale, mud to the knees, with bloody bandages untouched since put on days before; many bundled up in blankets, coats being lost, or useless; and all wearing that disheartened look which proclaimed defeat." These men had undergone a difficult, often excruciating, journey to arrive at the hospital. Typically, a wounded soldier was first taken to the rear, out of the line of fire; then perhaps transported to a field hospital (a tent) near the battlefield; then to a building, such as a farmhouse, that had quickly been converted for use as a hospital; then finally to a general hospital, such as the Union Hotel Hospital, in a major city. Transportation was by ambulance, but the ambulance system early in the war was remarkably crude, consisting of springless, horse-drawn carts often ineptly driven by men with little expertise. Many men complained that being driven in such carts was worse than being in battle. Eventually, a more efficient Ambulance Corps was established, but at the time of the battle at Fredericksburg, this system was in transition.[41]

## HOSPITAL LIFE AND MEDICAL CARE

Before the wounded from Fredericksburg arrived at Hurly-burly House, Alcott spent her first few days as a nurse taking care of a ward full of patients ill with "pneumonia on one side, diptheria on the other," and "five typhoids" opposite. This list of ailments reminds us that disease, rather than wounds, was in fact the chief killer during the Civil War. Of an estimated 620,000 men who died in the North and South, twice as many died as a result of disease than died in battle. Childhood diseases like measles and mumps, as well as smallpox, swept through army camps when troops gathered together early in the war. In addition, unsanitary living conditions, contaminated food and water, and mosquito bites led throughout the war to numerous "camp fevers" like typhoid, yellow fever, and malaria. Doctors during the Civil War did not understand the connections between water and typhoid or between mosquitoes and malaria. As a result, camp fevers resulted in 46,290 deaths among Union troops; diarrhea and dysentery accounted for another 44,558 Union deaths.[42]

But as Alcott confessed, she found little "romance" in caring for men with fever in wartime. She admitted that, "having a taste for 'ghastliness,'" she "rather longed for the wounded to arrive," since nursing men with rheumatism "wasn't heroic," and even nursing men with fever "had lost its charms since 'bathing burning brows'" (a phrase in fact typical of the kind of high-wrought potboilers Alcott wrote) "had been used up in romances, real and ideal." The reality of nursing was quite different, of course, as Nurse Periwinkle—Alcott's alter ego in *Hospital Sketches*—soon discovered; in first entering a room of wounded men, for instance, she confessed that she was met by "a regiment of the vilest odors that ever assaulted the human nose." As another nurse, Georgeanna Woolsey, concluded in an 1864 series of articles titled "How I Came to Be a Nurse," nursing was simply not appropriate for "a delicate creature whose head is full only of the romance of the work."[43]

The realities of hospital life were often grim, as modern readers will quickly discover even from Periwinkle's largely cheerful account. Admittedly, Periwinkle did not describe, as some observers did, maggot-infested wounds or the piles of stiffened limbs found outside amputation tents. Writing in wartime for a home-front audience, she instead spoke somewhat circumspectly of the "torn and shattered" men arriving on stretchers. Other female observers writing during and soon after the war were more graphic, describing men "in every condition of horror, borne, shattered and shrieking, by thoughtless hands, who banged the stretchers against pillars and posts, dumped them anywhere, and walked over the men without compassion."[44]

Yet Periwinkle certainly revealed, both inadvertently and purposefully, the primitive conditions of mid-nineteenth-century medical practice. At a time when the germ theory of infection had not yet gained acceptance, for instance, Periwinkle thought nothing of wetting successive soldiers' wounds by reusing one sponge and a basin of water—standard medical practice at the time. In the 1850s, Louis Pasteur had begun research in France that would eventually result in an understanding of the role of microorganisms in disease, but this knowledge had not yet made its way across the Atlantic.[45]

Surgeons, too, had no understanding of the importance of cleanliness during operations and did not wash beforehand or sterilize their instruments. As one surgeon remembered, "We operated in old blood-stained and often pus-stained coats [with] undisinfected hands" and "used undisinfected instruments from undisinfected plush-lined cases, and still worse used marine sponges which had been used in prior pus cases and had been only washed in tap water." No wonder, then, that a wounded Civil War soldier was more than eight times more likely to die of his wounds than a soldier injured in World War I. As James M. McPherson has put it, "the Civil War was fought at the end of the medical Middle Ages."[46]

One advance in surgery was the use of ether or chloroform as a form of anaesthesia; ether had first been used in 1846, while chloroform began to be used in 1851. However, as Periwinkle critically noted, while ether was typically administered to men undergoing amputations, "the merciful magic of ether was not thought necessary" for men undergoing the painful probing of wounds with sharp instruments—ample reason why, while a surgeon proceeded "to poke about among bits of bone and visible muscles," his patient "fainted quietly away."[47]

Surgeons prescribed "special diets" for men suffering from a variety of ailments, but the mid-nineteenth-century understanding of appropriate hospital diet was odd, even bizarre, by modern standards. Jane Stuart Woolsey remembered in her postwar memoir, *Hospital Days,* a typical "special diet" prescribed for a private with chronic diarrhea:[48]

| BREAKFAST | DINNER | SUPPER |
| --- | --- | --- |
| Coffee | Roast Beef | Oyster Soup |
| Steak | Fish | Raw Cabbage |
| Eggs | Radishes | Cheese |
| Bread | Boiled Cabbage | Bread |
| Butter | Bread | Butter |
| Milk-punch | Tea | Coffee |

For "inflammation of the stomach," another private was prescribed "hot cakes, cheese and molasses candy." Such diets revealed that the science of nutrition was little understood at the time of the war.[49]

Standard hospital practice left much to be desired in other ways, as well. Not only were convalescing soldiers employed to do work they were ill-fitted or too weak to do, but attendants employed for heavy labor or to take care of medical supplies were sometimes drunk, and crucial supplies often ran out or could not be found. As Alcott noted about one attendant in her ward who was asleep on the job, "he had been out that day, and whiskey asserted its supremacy in balmy whiffs." Within the hospital, disorganization was common, which was not surprising given that on the eve of the war the entire Army Medical Department had consisted only of a surgeon general, thirty surgeons, and eighty-three assistant surgeons. By the end of the war, some 12,000 doctors had served the Union, but the creation of a smooth-running hospital system was a monumental, ongoing task.[50]

Within the world of the hospital, what were the typical duties of the
female nurse? She had to answer to her hospital matron and to the
surgeon in charge of her ward for her assigned tasks. Primarily, as
Jane E. Schultz comments, "the average nurse was responsible for
washing, dressing, and feeding her patients." In addition, in "Union
general hospitals, nurses took charge of linen rooms and, in addition
to changing bedding, they were sometimes responsible for doing laun-
dry." Nurses also wrote letters for their patients or read to them. The
nurse Emily Elizabeth Parsons was one of a number of nurses who
made a careful record of her duties in letters home, giving us a vivid
sense of a typical nurse's day and a useful comparison to Alcott's
account.[51]

"My day begins early," Parsons said, "reveille at six, I must be up
before to get beds made, ward swept out, dressings attended to, and
wounds unbandaged and washed ready for the surgeon's inspection."
Parsons prepared "on plates the breakfast for each man on sick-
rations according to the rules the Doctor has written out in his order-
book for me." The doctor visited her ward every morning, and she
was in charge of making sure "that the baskets containing various
applications and dressings and the table the Doctor uses are standing
in a particular place in the ward; the basins with sponges and the pails
with hot and cold water in their places." She was then required to be
in attendance on the doctor as he performed his surgical work, in case
he needed supplies. These medical duties completed, she then prepared dinner [the mid-day meal] for her patients, and after dinner,
took care of "some housekeeping matters," including "counting out
the linen for forty-five men" and a thorough house-cleaning that one
day revealed "a whiskey bottle under one bed, apple pie on a table,
both delinquencies." Again she prepared a meal, supper, and after supper saw that the patients were "attended to properly" before putting
the ward's surgical baskets in order, including rolling up bandages.
Many of these duties, which also included writing letters, were duties
that women were familiar with at home. While there were slight varia-
tions on these duties among nurses, Parsons's account could nevertheless stand in for the experience of numerous nurses.[52]

Parsons was respectful of medical authority in her hospital and deferential to the surgeons under whom she worked. But not all nurses
were equally deferential, nor were all surgeons equally competent
or hospitals equally well administered. Georgeanna Woolsey, for instance, who worked for the U.S. Sanitary Commission, complained at

length that in the "Medical Department of the Army" a narrow "Professional Etiquette" held sway, what she called an "absolute Bogie" that "stands continually in one's path," showing "its narrow, ugly face" and which, "while not intentionally hard-hearted, would rather prefer to see a man die in the regular way, than to give him a chance of being saved irregularly." Particularly annoying to her was the way in which the "Bogie" of medical etiquette put "its cold paw on private benevolence." Slavish adherence to what were, in her view, illogical medical rules, was not in the best interest of the health of patients.[53]

A number of nurses made clear that they did not receive cordial treatment if they challenged doctors' orders or were seen to interfere with established custom in the army. And many women nurses resented being commanded by army surgeons whom they considered incompetent and callous. Yet Alcott seems to have had a more pleasant experience; indeed, her cordial relationships with doctors were an agreeable surprise, as she admitted that she "had been prepared by the accounts of others, to expect much humiliation of spirit from the surgeons, and to be treated by them like a door-mat, a worm, or any other meek and lowly article, whose mission it is to be put down and walked upon." Instead, she was "treated with the utmost courtesy and kindness." Periwinkle even felt emboldened to put aside her "carefully prepared meekness" and "more than once expressed a difference of opinion regarding sundry messes it was my painful duty to administer."[54]

Yet a number of doctors expressed frustration that women nurses, who had primarily gained their nursing expertise at home caring for family members, did not adhere to the military chain of command. In what was quintessentially a volunteer war, numerous civilians in fact simply arrived at hospitals or battlefields eager to help with the care of soldiers, without having been authorized to do so. One surgeon remembered such women volunteers with exasperation: "On the arrival of certain trains they would stalk into the office of district commanders, and establish themselves solemnly against the walls, entrenched behind their bags and parcels. They defied all military law." What's more, he complained sarcastically, they demanded service: "They did not wish much, not they, simply a room, a bed, a looking glass, someone to get their meals and do little things for them, and they would nurse the sick boys of our gallant Union Army." Many doctors also resented the presence of untrained nurses in hospitals. Periwinkle, for instance, like most other women nurses, apparently received no training whatsoever before beginning her work; instead, she took her "first lesson in the art of dressing wounds" simply by following a surgeon on his rounds.[55]

Nevertheless, a number of doctors, like many nurses themselves, assumed that women had special domestic skills they could bring to their work, and as a result, the doctors assigned some tasks by gender. Thus Dr. P. asked Periwinkle to tell one patient that he was dying, saying that "women have a way of doing such things comfortably, so I leave it to you." Moreover, soldiers themselves clearly appreciated the efforts of women nurses on their behalf: Emily Parsons noted of the soldiers in her care that "they seemed so glad to see me," and in a letter home, she reported that one soldier told her, "It is real cheery now, to have a woman come round one, it seems like home." One nurse, "Mother" Mary Ann Bickerdyke, achieved legendary status among soldiers as their tireless advocate with an often obtuse or uncaring medical establishment.[56]

Readers might be curious to know whether any record of Alcott's hospital service exists outside of her own writings. In fact, we get glimpses of Alcott at Hurly-burly House in the letters and journals of Hannah Ropes, the matron of the hospital, under whom she worked. "We are cheered by the arrival of Miss Alcott from Concord," Ropes wrote; Alcott offered "the prospect of a really good nurse, a gentlewoman who can do more than merely keep the patients from falling out of bed, as some of them seem to consider the whole duty of a nurse." Ropes's celebration of Alcott as a "gentlewoman" offered an implicit negative commentary on the many working-class women who in fact worked in hospitals during the war. Later, Ropes commented that "Miss Alcott and I worked together over four dying men and saved all but one," commenting that "she is a splendid young woman."[57]

On January 9, 1863, however, Ropes also commented that "we both have pneumonia and have suffered terribly"; Alcott had worked for only a few weeks before falling ill. Notified by telegram that his daughter was sick, Bronson Alcott arrived at the hospital on January 16, 1863. Finding her "ill of some hospital disease," he immediately decided "to bring her home while she is able to journey." She "persisted at first in staying longer," thinking it "ignominious to depart the post," her father noted; she later recorded that she was "very angry at first" when she saw him, as she knew it meant she "should have to go." Although her doctors attempted to "dissuade the effort" because of the seriousness of her condition and the possible danger of moving her, Bronson persisted: "I see not how she is to gain strength or spirits by remaining here," he wrote in his journal. His instincts proved right: Underlining the seriousness of Alcott's illness, Hannah Ropes died of typhoid fever at the Union Hotel Hospital on January 20, 1863. The next day, Louisa recorded, "I suddenly decided to go home, feeling very strangely & dreading to be worse." Miss Dix brought a basket for the journey "full of bottles of wine, tea, medicine, & cologne, beside a little blanket & pillow, a fan & a Testament." Two nurses accompanied them north, and Alcott finally arrived in Concord, "much enfeebled by her sickness and the long journey," on January 24, 1863. She recovered slowly: "Louisa comes down stairs to breakfast," was her father's sole notation in his journal for February 22. In late March, having had her head shaved on doctor's orders, she was only recently "up and about the house again, though weak and feeble."[58]

## THE CREATION OF *HOSPITAL SKETCHES*

Alcott not only kept a brief journal of her hospital experiences, but also wrote lengthy, vivid letters about her nursing to her family. "Letters come from Louisa giving lively descriptions of hospital scenes," Bronson Alcott noted in his journal. These letters, which have not survived, became the basis for a set of letters published serially in the Boston *Commonwealth* in the spring of 1863. Two editors of the *Commonwealth,* Frank Sanborn and Moncure Conway, an old family friend, had "teased" Alcott about the letters, suggesting that she arrange them "in a printable shape." The fact that her letters were circulated beyond her family revealed not only the close-knit nature of the Boston-Concord literary community, but also the intense interest that attached to all aspects of the war. "They thought them witty & pathetic, I didn't but I wanted money so I made three 'Hospital Sketches,'" she noted in her journal.[59]

She seems to have been genuinely astonished at the warm reception accorded her "sketches"; her surprise at this unexpected literary success echoes through her journals and letters. "Much to my surprise they made a great hit, & people bought the papers faster than they could be supplied," she commented in her journal; her sketches "were noticed, talked & inquired about much to my surprise & delight," she later reaffirmed. Because the "Sketches" were published serially, she was able to respond to some of the "inquiries" from "friendly readers" in a final "postscript" (the last chapter of the book). She was especially gratified that she received several letters of praise from men she admired. Henry James Sr., for instance, wrote to her of "how much pleasure" he had taken in her "charming pictures of hospital service" and "how refreshing he found the personal revelation there incidentally made of so much that is dearest & most worshipful in woman." A surgeon at the Union Hotel Hospital told her, "These papers have revealed to me much that is elevated, and pure, and refined in the soldiers' character, which I never before suspected. It is humiliating to me to think that I have been so long among them with such a mental or moral obtuseness that I never discovered it for myself."[60]

The experience of fame was new, gratifying, and perhaps a little unsettling. A year later, she noted that at a social gathering, people kept being brought to her "to be introduced till I was tired of shaking hands & hearing the words 'Hospital Sketches' uttered in every tone of interest, admiration, & respect." She found it "a very pleasant surprise & a new experience." "I liked it," she concluded, "but think a small dose quite as much as is good for me, for after sitting in a corner, & grubbing a la Cinderella it rather turns one's head to be taken out & treated like a Princess all of a sudden."[61]

Most gratifying of all were the two offers she received to publish the letters as a book; one from Roberts Brothers, who later published *Little Women,* and the other from James Redpath, a family acquaintance and prominent radical abolitionist who was beginning a new publishing venture. Redpath was himself an author who had published a book on John Brown on the eve of the war; now, given the intense interest shown in the war by the reading public, as well as the increasingly radical potential of the war in the wake of the January 1, 1863, Emancipation Proclamation, Redpath saw an opportunity to begin a new publishing firm. Given how much in tune she was with Redpath's radical politics, it is not surprising that Alcott chose to publish her book with him. Yet Redpath's fledgling publishing firm did not last long; it was only one of many ventures in the career of a restless intellectual who eventually became head of a prominent lecture bureau. Much later, Alcott reflected ruefully on her choice, saying, "Shortsighted Louisa! little did you dream that this same Roberts" was to "help you make your fortune a few years later. Redpath had no skill as a publisher & the Sketches never made much money."[62]

In 1863, however, Alcott was delighted with the offer from Redpath, negotiating the details of her contract in the self-deprecating manner that many women authors of the time adopted in order to maintain the cultural fiction that they inhabited a private, domestic sphere, even as they entered the public world of men and business. "Being lamentably stupid about business of all sorts," Alcott wrote to Redpath about her royalties, "I'm very much afraid I'm not very clear about the compact [contract]. But I believe stating it woman-fashion it means—I have five cents on each copy, you have ten to do what you like with & I'm not to meddle." Redpath advertised that he would devote five cents of every copy sold to "the support of orphans made fatherless or home-less by the war"; Alcott, financially pressed to take care of her father and mother—"for one possesses no gift for money making & the other is now too old to work"—could not make the equivalent gesture of charity, though "I should like to help the orphans," she said.[63]

Published in August 1863, *Hospital Sketches* was a "neat, green-covered 18mo. [an abbreviation indicating book size] of 100 pages, handsomely printed," and priced at fifty cents. The book included two chapters ("Obtaining Supplies" and "A Forward Movement") not pub-lished in the *Commonwealth,* but otherwise was much the same as the *Commonwealth* version. Alcott was thrilled with the book, writing to Redpath that "we all like the book very much, & I have the satisfaction of seeing my towns folk buying, reading, laughing & crying over it wherever I go." She was also pleased that Redpath "carried on the publishing of the Sketches vigorously, sending letters, proof & notices daily, & making all manner of offers, suggestions, & prophesies con-cerning the success of the book and its author." Showing an acute understanding of the literary marketplace despite her avowals to the contrary, Alcott provided Redpath with copies of letters of praise she received, which he promptly included in advertisements for the book. At the end of the year, reflecting on the success of *Hospital Sketches,* she mused that "I find I've done a good thing without knowing it."[64]

The first edition of *Hospital Sketches* was not large—only 1,000 copies. Although the book did not earn Alcott much money, it was still a distinct success, not only bringing Alcott into prominence, but also leading to numerous other offers. Redpath requested another book; the editor of the new *United States Service Magazine* asked for a story from her; and James T. Fields himself not only accepted a Civil War story, published as "The Brothers," but also asked if she had another book he might publish. Finally, Alcott was able to turn down an offer of employment as a teacher in a letter that must have given her great pleasure to write: "My time is fully occupied with my pen & I find story writing not only pleasanter than teaching but far more profitable," she told a would-be employer, "so I am glad to change the work which I have done for fifteen years for more congenial employment."[65]

In the fall of 1863, she reflected on her newfound success with amazement: "If ever there was an astonished young woman it is myself, for things have gone so swimmingly of late I don't know who I am. A year ago I had no publisher & went begging with my wares; now *three* have asked me for something, several papers are ready to print my contributions & F. B. S. [Sanborn of the *Commonwealth*] says 'any publisher this side Baltimore would be glad to get a book.' There is a sudden hoist for a meek & lowly scribbler who was told to 'stick to her teaching,' & never had a literary friend to lend a helping hand! Fifteen years of hard grubbing may be coming to something after all, & I may yet 'pay all the debts, fix the house, send May [her younger artistic sister, on whom Amy of *Little Women* was modeled] to Italy & keep the old folks cosy,' as I've said I would so long yet so hopelessly."[66]

In January 1864, she added up her accounts for the year past and found that "I have earned by my writing alone nearly six hundred dollars since last January, & spent less than a hundred for myself, which I am glad to know." She had become the main breadwinner in the family: "May has had $70 for herself, & the rest has paid debts or bought necessary things for the family," she noted. *Hospital Sketches* had launched her, at long last, on a successful writing career.[67]

## ALCOTT'S LITERARY STYLE

Alcott later noted that with *Hospital Sketches* she had discovered her "style," that engaging combination of poignant sentiment with drollery that would also delight readers of *Little Women*. In insisting on the importance of sentiment, Alcott was part of a larger middle-class culture of mid-nineteenth-century sentimentalism—what one scholar has called the "Sentimental Love Religion"—that emphasized the centrality of emotion, sympathy, and the "heart" in every individual's life. Although both men and women could (and did) adopt the sincere, heartfelt style of sentimentalism, it was middle-class white women who were primarily expected to be sentimentalists. As caretakers of the private, domestic realm, they were to provide for men a "haven from the heartless world" of public life; they were to act as both example and purifying influence through sincere, tender sensibility. This culture of sentimentalism was woven into every aspect of middle-class life in the mid-nineteenth century, including a vast print culture celebrating the "heart." The most widely read women's periodical of the day, *Godey's Lady's Book,* featured numerous articles stressing the importance of women's sentiment. *Uncle Tom's Cabin* (1852) also celebrated the power of sentiment, especially in a lengthy set-piece dramatizing the death of the child heroine little Eva. Thus it is not surprising that Alcott's *Hospital Sketches* was sometimes deeply sentimental as well; the chapter "A Night," in particular, offered a powerful rendering of a soldier's death that stressed the tender emotions of both the dying man and those who witnessed his death.[68]

But Alcott did not subscribe to all forms of literary sentimentalism, which included a range of literary styles and approaches. She was particularly critical of lugubrious sentimentalism that dwelled on dismal, melancholy, dreary emotions. (Such oppressively cheerless sentimentalism, a common style and mode of thought in the mid-nineteenth century, would later also be skewered by Mark Twain in *Huckleberry Finn.*) Alcott criticized the gloomy chaplain, for example, "who roamed vaguely about, informing the men that they were all worms, corrupt of heart, with perishable bodies." Instead, she offered a philosophy of cheerfulness and asserted the importance of humor throughout *Hospital Sketches.* It was a part of her "religion to look well after the cheerfulnesses of life," her narrator, Tribulation Periwinkle, affirmed in the last chapter. Indeed, she was proud of the fact that "I usually found my boys in the jolliest state of mind their condition allowed; for it was a known fact that Nurse Periwinkle objected to blue devils, and entertained a belief that he who laughed most was surest of recovery." She explicitly rejected the "'Hark!-from-the-tombs-a-doleful-sound' style of conversation" that "seemed to be the fashion." Instead, she embraced sympathy combined with humor, remaining always attuned to the "curious contrasts of the tragic and comic."[69]

In infusing *Hospital Sketches* with her love of the absurd, yet always remaining true to the sentimental ethos of the "heart," Alcott revealed her deep debt to Dickens, "the god of my idolatry." Dickens was enormously popular in mid-nineteenth-century America; Dickensian style—a brilliant mix of affectionate humor, grotesquerie, biting satire, pathos, and impassioned calls for social reform—was a striking influence on a wide range of authors, including Harriet Beecher Stowe. Alcott's love of Dickens—and his influence on her work—was evident throughout her life. That she read Dickens's works with attention and pleasure was clear throughout her letters and journals, in which she made frequent references to Dickens's characters. In the early 1850s, she and her sisters edited an amateur newspaper they called the *Pickwick Portfolio,* an explicit homage to

Dickens's *Pickwick Papers.* She also got up theatricals (another life-
long love) based on Dickens's novels; she had often played the character of Sairey Gamp in the sisters' childhood theatricals, and in the
middle of the war she wrote that she was "immensely busy just now
getting up some Scenes from Dickens for the benefit of the Fifty fifth
colored regiment." Later in the war, she put together another "Scenes
from Dickens" for the Sanitary Commission Fair in Boston. Thus it is
not surprising that *Hospital Sketches* itself began with an epigraph
from Sairey Gamp, a nurse in Dickens's *Martin Chuzzlewit,* or that the
name Alcott chose for her narrator, Tribulation Periwinkle, not only
had a typically Dickensian comic ring, it contained within it a reference to Mr. Winkle, one of Dickens's most famous characters from
*Pickwick Papers.*[70]

Alcott even used Dickens as a tool for healing. When she became a
nurse, she took volumes of Dickens with her to read to the soldiers, a
way of putting her philosophy of cheerfulness into action at even soldiers' most painful moments. When the "little Sergeant" had his "poor
arm" bandaged, for instance, he told Periwinkle, "I'd rather laugh than
cry, when I must sing out anyhow, so just say that bit from Dickens
again, please, and I'll stand it like a man." Periwinkle reported with
satisfaction that he did "stand it": "For 'Mrs. Cluppins,' 'Chadband,'
and 'Sam Weller,' [characters from *Pickwick Papers* and *Bleak House*]
always helped him through; thereby causing me to lay another offering of love and admiration on the shrine of the god of my idolatry."[71]

## CLAIMING A PLACE FOR WOMEN
## IN THE WAR EFFORT

Dickens may have inspired Alcott, but she also created her own lively
style in *Hospital Sketches* to express concerns often defined by her
position as a single woman. "I want something to do," her narrator
cried in the opening sentence (just as Alcott did in her own journals)
before rejecting the obvious choices before her, including teaching
and marriage. To her sister's suggestion that she "take a husband like
my Darby, and fulfill your mission," Periwinkle responded with a drop
of acid typical of Alcott's approach: "Can't afford expensive luxuries."
Although Alcott could not become a soldier, in telling the story of her
nursing she militarized the language she employed, thus creating a
metaphoric equivalence with soldiers. "I've enlisted!" she told her family, and then "turned military at once, called my dinner my rations,

saluted all new comers, and ordered a dress parade that very afternoon." Spinning this metaphor out, Alcott even applied military language to the most feminized of Tribulation's own activities and
concerns: the washing and mending of her clothing. "Having reviewed
every rag I possessed," Periwinkle said, "I detailed some for picket
duty while airing over the fence; some to the sanitary influences of the
wash-tub; others to mount guard in the trunk; while the weak and
wounded went to the Work-basket Hospital, to be made ready for active service again."[72]

Military service was one of the central metaphors of the volume, a
means of claiming (although always with a gesture of self-deprecating
humor) a central place in the war for women. But there were other
important structuring devices in the volume as well, including the idea
of journeys both literal and metaphoric—travels through space but
also travels into new forms of knowledge and experience. The first
chapters of *Hospital Sketches,* "Obtaining Supplies" and "A Forward
Movement," for example (whose titles maintained the reigning military metaphor of the volume), detailed Periwinkle's literal journey
south to Washington. But this literal journey was also a metaphoric
journey, one that took Periwinkle out of her accustomed sphere within
the domestic realm into a new sphere of public life.

An underlying concern of *Hospital Sketches*—and a vexed question
for Alcott in her own life—was not only what constituted appropriate
behavior in public for women, but to what extent she had to bow to
the restrictive gender conventions of her day. Alcott never openly
rebelled against such conventions (by becoming a cross-dressing soldier, for instance), but she did express a continual awareness of them
and often chafed against them. On her journey south, for instance,
after having finally obtained her pass, she commented, "having heard
complaints of the absurd way in which American women become
images of petrified propriety, if addressed by strangers, when traveling alone, the inborn perversity of my nature" caused "me to assume
an entirely opposite style of deportment." "I put my bashfulness in my
pocket," and plunged into a long conversation with a stranger "on the
war, the weather, music, Carlyle, skating, genius, hoops and the immortality of the soul." With such humor she expressed disapproval of
forms of propriety she considered stifling.[73]

Through humor she could also express anger without becoming
"shrill" or "shrewish," those gendered adjectives so often applied to
women who expressed negative feelings. When Periwinkle was turned
away by an unhelpful, taciturn functionary at the State House, she

imagined acting on her anger—but avoided the impropriety of actually doing so. If "I could have shaken this negative gentleman vigorously, the relief would have been immense," she commented, but "the prejudices of society forbidding this mode of redress, I merely glowered at him." Her failed attempt to navigate an unyielding bureaucracy over the course of a day reminded her of her difficult position as a woman: "I'm a woman's rights woman," she said, referring to the mid-nineteenth-century women's reform movement, which included a demand for woman's suffrage, "and if any man had offered help in the morning, I should have condescendingly refused it, sure that I could do everything as well, if not better, myself. My strong-mindedness had rather abated since then, and I was now quite ready to be a 'timid trembler,' if necessary." She in fact enlisted the help of her brother-in-law before finally succeeding in her goal of obtaining a free railroad pass south to Washington. As the two opening chapters show, it was difficult for any civilian to navigate the red tape (a term that became popular during the war) involved in getting to the front during the war, but it was especially difficult for women.[74]

Of course, the greatest conundrum facing a young, middle-class white woman becoming a nurse was not travel but the basic paradox of her job: that the care of men's (often naked) bodies, which lay at the heart of the job of nursing wounded soldiers, was itself a breach of propriety. Alcott was typically humorous on this point. After the novice nurse Periwinkle was given the "appalling directions" to wash the soldiers under her care, she commented that if she had been requested "to shave them all, or dance a hornpipe on the stove funnel, I should have been less staggered; but to scrub some dozen lords of creation at a moment's notice, was really—really——." "However," she concluded, "there was no time for nonsense, and, having resolved when I came to do everything I was bid, I drowned my scruples in my washbowl, clutched my soap manfully, and, assuming a business-like air, made a dab at the first dirty specimen I saw."[75]

Clutching soap "manfully" and being "business-like" were both ways of dealing with the improprieties of caring for men's bodies by claiming nonfeminine attributes. But the most powerful means by which Alcott justified nursing within *Hospital Sketches* was through claiming maternal and domestic authority over her patients. Civil War America was in fact a deeply maternalist culture, which placed mothers at the emotional center of the household and placed great value on the virtues of home. Civil War popular literature reflected this maternalism, often celebrating soldiers' connections to their mothers. Indeed, as Oliver Wendell Holmes noted, the most popular songs of the Civil War, some selling upwards of 500,000 copies, were sentimental songs with the word "mother" in their titles, such as "Just Before the Battle, Mother," or "Who Will Care for Mother Now?"[76]

Thus the most compelling argument that women could make to justify nursing strangers was that in doing so they brought the virtues of home to the battlefront and hospital. Tribulation Periwinkle stressed the maternal nature of her feelings for wounded soldiers under her care, rather than reminding readers that she was a single woman among (often) single men. She had "a womanly pride in their regard, a motherly affection for them all," she commented. When the soldiers arrived from Fredericksburg, Periwinkle asserted that it was "the matron's motherly face" that "brought more comfort to many a poor soul, than the cordial draughts she administered, or the cheery words that welcomed all, making of the hospital a home." And when Alcott portrayed Periwinkle washing soldiers, she emphasized that she "scrubbed away like any tidy parent on a Saturday night" and that some of the soldiers "took the performance like sleepy children, leaning their tired heads against me as I worked."[77]

If imagining nurses as mothers lessened the impropriety of coming into contact with strange men's bodies, then imagining soldiers as boys and children completed the metaphoric creation of surrogate families within the confines of the hospital. Throughout *Hospital Sketches* and in her letters as well, Alcott referred to soldiers as "our boys." She was not alone: Calling soldiers "boys" was a usage that arose during the Civil War, reflecting not just the youth of many soldiers, but also their perceived connection to the maternal culture of the home front as America's "sons." As Oliver Wendell Holmes commented in 1865, "these were *boys* then who fought our battles, boys at heart, if not always, as they often were, in years and growth."[78]

Many soldiers during the Civil War were of course literally boys. According to estimates made by Bell Irvin Wiley, for instance, approximately 1.6 percent of Union soldiers were under eighteen years old. Still, the point remains that, according to Wiley, "the great mass" of Union soldiers, approximately 98 percent, "were neither very old nor very young, but fell in the eighteen-to-forty-five group." James M. McPherson has commented that the median age of soldiers was 23.5. Yet imagining soldiers as "boys" became so commonplace during the conflict that it suggests a distinct cultural unease with the idea of soldiers as full-grown men separated from the maternalist culture of home. Certainly in *Hospital Sketches* it was through imagining soldiers as "boys" that the possible sexual threat of nursing was lessened.[79]

Nurse Periwinkle's motherly affection for the soldiers under her care was most compellingly displayed in the chapter that formed the emotional centerpiece of *Hospital Sketches,* "A Night," in which she witnessed the lingering death of John, a noble Virginia blacksmith. Shot through the lungs, John was an ideal type of American manhood: "A most attractive face he had, framed in brown hair and beard, comely featured and full of vigor," with a mouth "grave and firm, with plenty of will and courage in its lines."[80]

But at first Nurse Periwinkle did not recognize John's need for maternal affection and found his obvious manliness disquieting. She "was a little afraid of the stately looking man, whose bed had to be lengthened to accommodate his commanding stature; who seldom spoke, uttered no complaint," and "asked no sympathy." It was only when John inadvertently revealed his emotional, tender, childish side by crying, that Periwinkle responded to him fully. "I had forgotten," Periwinkle said, "that the strong man might long for the gentler tendance of a woman's hands, the sympathetic magnetism of a woman's presence, as well as the feebler souls about him." Noticing John looking "lonely and forsaken," she saw "great tears roll down and drop upon the floor." Now she was able to respond to him not as a self-sufficient man, but as a boy: "My fear vanished, my heart opened wide and took him in," and she gathered "the bent head in my arms, as freely as if he had been a little child."[81]

Periwinkle's account stressed John's boyish qualities. Although he was almost thirty and "the manliest man" among the patients Nurse Periwinkle cared for, he also said " 'Yes, ma'am,' like a little boy," and "his eyes were child's eyes, looking one fairly in the face." As Alcott made clear, it was only through recognizing John's powerless, enfeebled, boyish qualities that Periwinkle could fully celebrate him as a soldier. Afraid of the manly man, she was tender and compassionate with the homesick, yearning boy.[82]

Readers who wonder whether such a soldier existed will be interested to know that the portrayal of John was based on a soldier under Alcott's care named John Sulie. His dignified, attractive qualities also deeply affected the hospital matron Hannah Ropes, who wrote an extended account of his death in her journal. In a number of ways, Ropes's and Alcott's accounts were similar: Both emphasized John's manliness and dignity for instance, with Ropes writing in her journal that "there he lay, his broad chest heaving with obstinate breath, but the face as composed in its manly beauty, as though he were taking natural rest in sleep. The dignity of the man, considering the circumstances, was wonderful." Ropes recorded as well the haunting detail that just hours before his death, Sulie "reached his right hand into Miss Alcott's lap and firmly grasped her wrist."[83]

Yet the two accounts also diverged in ways that have much to tell us about Alcott's artistry within a larger sentimental wartime culture. Ropes made clear in her account that Sulie said little as he neared death: "He could not talk but a word at a time." She also indicated that she was alone with him at the moment of death: "The matron is left alone when the breath ceases." Yet his "wondrous manly beauty" in death so impressed her that she sent an "attendant to call Miss Alcott back" to gaze upon his body.[84]

Alcott's rendering of John's death drew on such poignant details but also attempted to give meaning to his death within the parameters of sentimental literary culture. One of the central problems posed by the war was the shocking anonymity of the suffering and death undergone by ordinary soldiers far from home. Mid-nineteenth-century Americans hoped to achieve "good deaths," which included communicating their last thoughts to loved ones gathered at their bedsides and, within a deeply religious culture, achieving a final reconciliation with God. Anonymous death was an aspect of war that many Americans found unbearable; they simply could not accept that soldiers' deaths would occur without tender friends and family members in attendance.[85]

But as Alcott made clear in *Hospital Sketches,* it was not often possible for family members to be present at the deathbeds of their sons, husbands, or brothers in wartime. Not even chaplains could be at the deathbeds of every soldier. To a "friendly reader" who inquired whether there were religious "services by hospital death-beds," Alcott observed that "the men died, and were carried away, with as little ceremony as on a battlefield." Registering indignation at this fact of war, she wrote of a soldier who asked her for a drink of water, and who died before she could give it to him: "It seemed a poor requital for all he had sacrificed and suffered,—that hospital bed, lonely even in a crowd; for there was no familiar face for him to look his last upon; no friendly voice to say, Good bye; no hand to lead him gently down into the Valley of the Shadow; and he vanished, like a drop in that red sea upon whose shores so many women stand lamenting. For a moment I felt bitterly indignant at this seeming carelessness of the value of life, the sanctity of death." For Alcott, as for other Civil War writers like Walt Whitman, it was a cultural affront that wartime death occurred outside of the framework of sentimental norms that emphasized a tender, emotive parting from family and friends.[86]

Thus "A Night" worked instead to portray a "good death" for John, in which he was able to express his last thoughts, write home, and say a tender farewell to a comrade. While John Sulie apparently died in the middle of the night, Alcott instead represented her noble black-smith as having died at dawn, thus allowing her to give an implicit religious meaning to his death. After suffering greatly at the last, he saw "the first red streak of dawn" and "seemed to read in it a sign of hope of help, for, over his whole face there broke that mysterious expression, brighter than any smile, which often comes to eyes that look their last." This last evocation of the dawn, a conventional mode of rendering sentimental death, allowed Alcott to suggest that John's sufferings might be the vehicle to ultimate redemption, thus keeping John's death within the parameters of the "sentimental love religion."[87]

The fact that Alcott used sentimental literary conventions to portray John's death did not mean, of course, that she was any less sincerely moved by his death. Like other authors writing during the Civil War, she necessarily worked within the literary conventions available to her. Walt Whitman, too, created "sentimental soldiers" within his wartime writings, and numerous other observers joined Alcott in writing sympathetic accounts of hospitalized soldiers that included short stories, articles, and full-length books like the 1864 *Notes of Hospital Life*. Such observers assumed—quite correctly—that a home-front reading public would be interested in their accounts of the war.

Indeed, given that a highly developed commercial literary market-place existed at the time of the war, many observers believed that their accounts might have commercial as well as patriotic value. The hospital matron Hannah Ropes, for instance, hoped in the winter of 1862 that the Boston *Advertiser* "would send me a *good price*" for excerpts from her journal. As she and others knew, there was intense interest on the part of the reading public in firsthand accounts of "our boys" in wartime. Moreover, hospital visitors and nurses realized that they had knowledge of the war that civilians on the home front lacked. Many, including Alcott, traced their own journeys from romantic preconceptions to more realistic understandings of the war—and, by extension, life more generally—through their work.[88]

## THE SOCIAL LANDSCAPE OF THE HOSPITAL

Periwinkle's relationships with other workers in Hurly-burly House provide interesting insights into the ways in which gender, class, race, and professional status mapped the social geography of hospitals.

During the war, thousands of African American and white working-class women were employed as laundresses, cooks, and nurses in hospitals, but these workers often appear only in passing, quite literally, in *Hospital Sketches*. Going up the stairs of Hurly-burly House, for instance, Periwinkle noted that she was "hopelessly entangled in a knot of colored sisters coming to wash." African American women workers are otherwise largely invisible in the text. While Periwinkle complained that "the nurses were willing to be served by the colored people, but seldom thanked them, never praised, and scarcely recognized them in the street," her own text ironically replicated that neglect, providing individuality only to the African American waiter Isaac, who prevented her from being served dinner one evening.[89]

*Hospital Sketches* reveals that Alcott's racial attitudes were complicated in ways typical of numerous Northern white abolitionists. On the one hand, she enthusiastically supported emancipation, writing that at the turn of midnight on New Year's Eve 1863, as the Emancipation Proclamation went into effect, Periwinkle "electrified" her roommate by "dancing out of bed, throwing up the window, and flapping my handkerchief, with a feeble cheer, in answer to the shout of a group of colored men in the street below." She also "daily shocked some neighbor by treating the blacks as [she] did the whites," including kissing a "funny little black baby" to the shock of a "Virginia woman" nearby.[90]

Yet the very way in which Periwinkle theatrically described such physical contact underlines the "romantic racialism" that permeates *Hospital Sketches*. Like Harriet Beecher Stowe, Alcott infantilized African Americans, viewing them as "the sort of creatures generations of slavery have made them: obsequious, trickish, lazy and ignorant, yet kind-hearted" and "merry-tempered." She viewed African Americans through a set of lenses shaped by popular fiction and minstrelsy. On her journey to Washington, for instance, she commented that "we often passed colored people looking as if they had come out of a picture book, or off the stage, but not at all the sort of people I'd been accustomed to see at the North." Periwinkle's animalistic phrasing also revealed layers of racism: She described a six-year-old "contraband," for instance, as an "imp" who "scuttled away"; she almost stepped on a baby who was underfoot "like a little black spider." Aware of her own racial prejudices, Periwinkle "expected to have to defend [herself] from accusations of a prejudice against color." However, in the end, Periwinkle "was surprised to find things just the other way" and discovered that men "would put two *gs* into negro, and scoff at the idea of any good coming from such trash." The prejudices of those around her were virulent indeed.[91]

While some ambivalence underlay Alcott's portrayals of African Americans, little such ambivalence informed her depictions of white soldiers. They were, quite simply, heroes—but heroes, strikingly, without any trappings of military pomp or grandeur. Indeed, Periwinkle celebrated the very ordinariness of her "brave boys," who were far from being the romantic, bayonet-charging heroes of numerous engravings and poems during the war. These were not men who boasted about their military feats; instead, their bravery consisted in coping cheerfully with often desperate wounds. The little Sergeant, for instance, had "one leg gone, and the right arm so shattered that it must evidently follow," yet "was as merry as if his afflictions were not worth lamenting over." And they had ordinary, not "heroic," concerns. Another soldier worried about what "Josephine Skinner" at home would say about a prominent scar on his cheek.[92]

Alcott's soldiers revealed a tender concern for one another that brought into sharp relief the question of what constituted appropriate masculinity in wartime. In her portrayal, the close comradeship among soldiers allowed for loving, affectionate relationships with a quasi-feminine quality: "They kissed each other, tenderly as women," she noted, for instance, about the two friends Ned and John as they said a final goodbye. Without making the point explicitly, Alcott pointed to the possibility that war empowered men to express emotions they might not be allowed to reveal in peacetime. *Hospital Sketches* thus raises interesting questions about the impact of war on norms of masculinity and femininity. While some might argue that war always produces more exaggerated, even rigid gender stereotyping, *Hospital Sketches* seems to suggest that during the Civil War, norms of masculinity and femininity were mutable, flexible, and even interchangeable.[93]

Early in the war, a number of writers had celebrated the heroism of high-ranking officers, not sergeants or members of the "ranks." But Alcott instead found heroism in the ordinary soldiers under her care, whom she portrayed with affection and humor. She was not alone in doing so: Hannah Ropes simply said "the heroes are in the ranks." And as another nurse wrote in her anonymously published 1864 *Notes of Hospital Life,* "at the opening of the war" she had thought "that the finer feelings of our nature were exclusively the property of the higher classes." But two years as a nurse in a military hospital, "where men appear mentally as well as physically in 'undress uniform,'" had shown her "the utter fallacy of such a theory." She dedicated her volume "to the Privates of the Army of the United States."[94]

By the middle of the war, a number of writers had claimed heroism for the hospital, not just the battlefield. A. S. Hooker's "Hospital Heroes," for instance, published in 1863 in the popular weekly *Frank Leslie's Illustrated Newspaper,* denied that "all the heroes" were on the battlefield, instead asserting that "our hospitals are full of heroes," who "uncomplaining die." As Anna Holstein wrote in her 1867 *Three Years in Field Hospitals of the Army of the Potomac,* Union soldiers endured "suffering with a heroism which exceeds even the bravery of the battle-field." The author William Howell Reed, too, noted this "harder heroism of the hospital." Part of that "harder heroism" involved the aftereffects of battle, and Alcott was unusually truthful in recording the lingering psychological effects of battle, portraying men in states of delirium and mental disturbance, as they restlessly and feverishly relived the awful stresses of battle in the still of the night.[95]

Strikingly, Alcott's hospital heroes came from many walks of American life and included an "Irishman" and a "big Prussian, who spoke no English." Like other wartime writers, Alcott used ethnic and regional stereotypes in portraying these and other soldiers, associating Irish soldiers, for instance, with a particular style of humor. Nevertheless, in deliberately including a diverse group of men in her narrative, Alcott also imagined a diverse nationhood, one whose symbolic heart could be found in the hospital itself.[96]

## *HOSPITAL SKETCHES* AND THE MEANINGS OF THE CIVIL WAR

*Hospital Sketches* was part of an outpouring of war literature published during the Civil War, writing that bore the complicated traces of commercial democracy. Like numerous other wartime authors, Alcott hoped to earn a livelihood from her writings, thus combining patriotism with practicality. This aim did not make *Hospital Sketches* less meaningful, but it does remind us that literature is not created in a commercial vacuum. After all, other writers, too, shared Alcott's commercial hope. In the wake of her success, in fact, Walt Whitman made a proposal to her publisher, James Redpath, for "a book of the time, worthy the time—something considerably beyond mere hospital sketches—a book for sale perhaps in a larger American market—the premises or skeleton memoranda of incidents, persons, places, sights, the past year." Whitman noted that he especially had "much to say of the hospitals," including "many hospital incidents" that "will take with the general reader." He concluded that his book "should be got out *immediately.* I think an edition, elegantly bound, might be pushed off for books for presents etc. for the holidays, if advertised for that purpose. It would be very appropriate. I think it a book that would please women. I should expect it to be popular with the trade."[97]

Whitman did not publish his book in wartime, but numerous other hospital observers, including many women, recorded their experiences both during and after the war. They knew that civilians on the homefront were eager to read about the experiences of their "brave boys"; indeed, even some of those brave boys themselves apparently read Alcott's account with interest. The nurse Amanda Akin Stearns recorded in her diary of December 6, 1863, that "when evening came" she sat next to one of her soldier patients "to keep him from feeling lonely and dispirited" at a time when "thoughts of home came very sweet and its comforts seemed very far off." She then "read aloud a chapter from Miss Alcott's 'Hospital Sketches,'" which seemed to entertain a number very much, particularly my sensible John," who said "he did not see where such an interesting book came from; he had not been able to get such and would like to buy it."[98]

It is not hard to see why this soldier might have enjoyed reading *Hospital Sketches,* with its humorous, telling, and often sharp-tongued observations of hospital life. We, too, can continue to enjoy Alcott's winning combination of sympathy and appreciation for the absurd. But *Hospital Sketches* has more to teach us, as well: It reminds us that during the Civil War, many Americans, including women, believed that the deepest meanings of war lay in the wounded bodies of individual soldiers, who made an abstract nationhood powerfully concrete.

## NOTES

[1] Caps, often worn with a cockade (ribbon) on the side.

[2] Louisa May Alcott, *The Journals of Louisa May Alcott,* ed. Joel Myerson, Daniel Shealy, and Madeleine B. Stern (Boston: Little, Brown, 1989), 105, cited hereafter as *Journals;* and Louisa May Alcott, *The Selected Letters of Louisa May Alcott,* ed. Joel Myerson, Daniel Shealy, and Madeleine B. Stern (Boston: Little, Brown, 1987), 64, cited hereafter as *Letters.*

[3] Biographies of Alcott include Ednah D. Cheney, *Louisa May Alcott: Her Life, Letters, and Journals* (Boston: Roberts Bros., 1889); Sarah Elbert, *A Hunger for Home: Louisa May Alcott and Little Women* (Philadelphia: Temple University Press, 1984; rev. ed., New Brunswick, N.J.: Rutgers University Press, 1987); Martha Saxton, *Louisa May: A Mod-*

*ern Biography* (New York: Avon, 1978); and Madeleine B. Stern, *Louisa May Alcott* (Norman: University of Oklahoma Press, 1950). See also Elaine Showalter, "Introduction," *Alternative Alcott: Louisa May Alcott* (New Brunswick, N.J.: Rutgers University Press, 1988). On the Alcott family, see Madelon Bedell, *The Alcotts: Biography of a Family* (New York: Clarkson N. Potter, 1980). On Civil War popular literature, see Alice Fahs, *The Imagined Civil War: Popular Literature of the North and South, 1861–1865* (Chapel Hill: University of North Carolina Press, 2001). On Northern women writers during the war, see especially Lyde Cullen Sizer, *The Political Work of Northern Women Writers and the Civil War, 1850–1872* (Chapel Hill: University of North Carolina Press, 2000); and Elizabeth Young, *Disarming the Nation: Women's Writings and the American Civil War* (Chicago: University of Chicago Press, 1999). See also Daniel Aaron, *The Unwritten War: American Writers and the Civil War* (New York: Knopf, 1973); Louis P. Masur, ed., *"The Real War Will Never Get in the Books": Selections from Writers during the Civil War* (New York: Oxford University Press, 1993); and Edmund Wilson, *Patriotic Gore: Studies in the Literature of the American Civil War* (New York: Oxford University Press, 1966).

[4]*Journals,* 69, 88, 100.

[5]On Bronson Alcott, see Frederick C. Dahlstrand, *Amos Bronson Alcott: An Intellectual Biography* (Rutherford, N.J.: Fairleigh Dickinson University Press, 1982); and Odell Shepard, *Pedlar's Progress: The Life of Bronson Alcott* (Boston: Little, Brown, 1937). On Transcendentalism, see especially Louis Menand, *The Metaphysical Club: A Story of Ideas in America* (New York: Farrar, Straus and Giroux, 2001).

[6]*Journals,* 71.

[7]*Journals,* 103.

[8]*Journals,* 61, 65, 69, 90.

[9]*Journals,* 67, 79.

[10]Rebecca Harding Davis, *Bits of Gossip* (Boston: Houghton Mifflin, 1904), 38–39. Similarly, in 1860 Alcott recorded that she had been "asked to the John Brown meeting, but had no 'good gown,' so didn't go" (*Journals,* 101).

[11]On the ideology of separate spheres, see especially Nancy Cott, *The Bonds of Womanhood: "Woman's Sphere" in New England, 1780–1835* (New Haven, Conn.: Yale University Press, 1977); and Barbara Leslie Epstein, *The Politics of Domesticity: Women, Evangelism, and Temperance in Nineteenth-Century America* (Middletown, Conn.: Wesleyan University Press, 1981). On the problems facing middle-class women writers, see Mary Kelley, *Private Woman, Public Stage: Literary Domesticity in Nineteenth-Century America* (New York: Oxford University Press, 1984); and Ann Douglas, *The Feminization of American Culture* (New York: Knopf, 1977). On middle-class life more generally in mid-nineteenth-century America, see Stuart M. Blumin, *The Emergence of the Middle Class: Social Experience in the American City, 1760–1900* (New York: Cambridge University Press, 1989); and Anne C. Rose, *Victorian America and the Civil War* (Cambridge: Cambridge University Press, 1992). *Journals,* 108, 69; Bronson Alcott, *Letters,* 183; *Journals,* 71, 108, 94.

[12]*Journals,* 78.

[13]Alice Kessler-Harris, *Out to Work: A History of Wage-Earning Women in the United States* (New York: Oxford University Press, 1982), 75, 79. On the Civil War's effects on working women and sewing women in particular, see Kessler-Harris, 75–83.

[14]*Journals,* 78, 71.

[15]*Journals,* 73, 90.

[16]*Journals,* 73, 85, 92, 95. On literary ambition among women, see Kelley, *Private Woman, Public Stage.*

[17]*Letters,* 75, 57.

[18]On Fields, see William S. Tryon, *Parnassus Corner: A Life of James T. Fields, Publisher to the Victorians* (Boston: Houghton Mifflin, 1963). *Letters,* 73. Fields's wife was distantly related to the Alcotts. For the relationship between the two families, see *Letters,* 85. On James Redpath, see Madeleine B. Stern, *Imprints on History: Book Publishers and*

*American Frontiers* (Bloomington: Indiana University Press, 1956), 76–83; and Charles F. Horner, *The Life of James Redpath and the Development of the Modern Lyceum* (New York: Barse & Hopkins, 1926).

[19] *Journals*, 109, 111, footnote. See also *Journals*, 121.

[20] *Letters*, 67, 72.

[21] For the phrase "blood & thunder," see *Journals*, 132. On Alcott's sensational writings, see especially Louisa May Alcott, *Louisa May Alcott Unmasked: Collected Thrillers*, ed. Madeleine B. Stern (Boston: Northeastern University Press, 1995); and Louisa May Alcott, *Freaks of Genius: Unknown Thrillers of Louisa May Alcott*, ed. Daniel Shealy, Madeleine B. Stern, and Joel Myerson (New York: Greenwood Press, 1991). On sensational writings more generally in mid-nineteenth-century America, see David S. Reynolds, *Beneath the American Renaissance: The Subversive Imagination in the Age of Emerson and Melville* (New York: Knopf, 1988). Margo Jefferson, "On Writers and Writing: D. H. Lawrence Frees the Slaves," *New York Times Book Review*, January 19, 2003, 23. *Journals*, 132, 109.

[22] *Journals*, 108–9.

[23] *Letters*, 64. On early war excitement in the North, see especially Philip S. Paludan, *A People's Contest: The Union and the Civil War, 1861–1865* (New York: Harper & Row, 1988).

[24] *Letters*, 66, 78–79.

[25] *Letters*, 92–93.

[26] On the women who crossed these gender boundaries by cross-dressing to become soldiers, see Elizabeth D. Leonard, *All the Daring of the Soldier: Women of the Civil War Armies* (New York: Norton, 1999); Sarah Rosetta Wakeman, *An Uncommon Soldier: The Civil War Letters of Sarah Rosetta Wakeman, Alias Private Lyons Wakeman, 153rd Regiment, New York State Volunteers, 1862-1864*, ed. Lauren Cook Burgess (New York: Oxford University Press, 1995); and DeAnne Blanton and Lauren M. Cook, *They Fought Like Demons: Women Soldiers in the American Civil War* (Baton Rouge: Louisiana State University Press, 2002). *Journals*, 105. *Letters*, 64. On women's work during the Civil War, see especially Jeanie Attie, *Patriotic Toil: Northern Women and the American Civil War* (Ithaca, N.Y.: Cornell University Press, 1998); Mary A. Livermore, *My Story of the War: The Civil War Memoirs of the Famous Nurse, Relief Organizer and Suffragette* (1887; reprint, New York: Da Capo, 1995); Mary Elizabeth Massey, *Women in the Civil War* (1966; reprint, Lincoln: University of Nebraska Press, 1994); Agatha Young, *The Women and the Crisis: Women of the North in the Civil War* (New York: McDowell, Bolensky, 1959); and Sylvia G. L. Dannett, *Noble Women of the North* (New York: T. Yoseloff, 1959). Two contemporary collections celebrating women's contributions to the war effort are Frank Moore, ed., *Women of the War: Their Heroism and Self-Sacrifice* (Hartford, Conn.: S. S. Scranton, 1866); and L. P. Brockett and Mary C. Vaughan, *Women's Work in the Civil War: A Record of Heroism, Patriotism, and Patience* (Philadelphia: Zeigler, McCurdy, 1867). See *Harper's Weekly*, June 29, 1861. See Alice Fahs, "The Feminized Civil War: Gender, Northern Popular Literature, and the Memory of the War, 1861-1900," *Journal of American History* 85 (March 1999): 1461–94. *Journals*, 105; *Letters*, 64.

[27] *Letters*, 64; *Journals*, 105.

[28] *Letters*, 80, 77. The correspondent was Thomas Wentworth Higginson, Colonel of the 1st South Carolina Volunteers, a black regiment. *Letters*, 96, 77.

[29] *Journals*, 45. Louisa May Alcott, *Hospital Sketches*, ed. Bessie Z. Jones (Cambridge, Mass.: Belknap Press, 1960), xiii. *Journals*, 95–96.

[30] *Letters*, 96; Journals 120, 131, 133, 122. *Hospital Sketches*, 119. (Note: Page numbers refer to pages in this text.)

[31] *Letters*, 65.

[32] On Civil War nursing, see Kristie Ross, "Arranging a Doll's House: Refined Women as Union Nurses," in *Divided Houses: Gender and the Civil War*, ed. Catherine Clinton

and Nina Silber (New York: Oxford University Press, 1992), 97–113; Jane E. Schultz, "'Are We Not All Soldiers?' Northern Women in the Civil War Hospital Service," *Prospects* 20 (1995): 39–56; Jane E. Schultz, "The Inhospitable Hospital: Gender and Professionalism in Civil War Medicine," *Signs* 17 (winter 1992): 363–92; Nina Bennett Smith, "The Women Who Went to the War: The Union Army Nurse in the Civil War" (Ph.D. diss., Northwestern University, 1981); Stephen B. Oates, *A Woman of Valor: Clara Barton and the Civil War* (New York: Free Press, 1994); and Elizabeth Leonard, *Yankee Women: Gender Battles in the Civil War* (New York: Norton, 1994). Henry Wadsworth Longfellow, "Santa Filomena," *Atlantic Monthly* 1 (Nov. 1857): 22–23.

[33]*Hospital Sketches,* 96. On Dorothea Dix, see David Gollaher, *Voice for the Mad: The Life of Dorothea Dix* (New York: Free Press, 1995).

[34]See James M. McPherson, *Battle Cry of Freedom: The Civil War Era* (New York: Oxford University Press, 1988), 480–84; and Attie, *Patriotic Toil,* 38–44. Schultz, "'Are We Not All Soldiers?'" 40–41.

[35]*Journals,* 106, 109.

[36]On Stevenson's career, see Hannah Ropes, *Civil War Nurse: The Diary and Letters of Hannah Ropes,* ed. John R. Brumgardt (Knoxville: University of Tennessee Press, 1980). Stevenson had helped Alcott obtain work as a seamstress at a desperate point in 1858. See *Journals,* 91. Oates, *A Woman of Valor,* 10. *Hospital Sketches,* ed. Bessie Z. Jones, xxvii. *Journals,* 116, 123.

[37]*Journals,* 110.

[38]*Hospital Sketches,* 97, 71.

[39]For accounts of the battle, see George C. Rable, *Fredericksburg! Fredericksburg!* (Chapel Hill: University of North Carolina Press, 2002); McPherson, *Battle Cry of Freedom,* 568–74; and Margaret E. Wagner, Gary W. Gallagher, and Paul Finkelman, eds., *The Library of Congress Civil War Desk Reference* (New York: Simon & Schuster, 2002), 271–74.

[40]Wagner et al., *Library of Congress Civil War Desk Reference,* 250.

[41]*Hospital Sketches,* 71. For more on the Ambulance Corps, see Wagner et al., *Library of Congress Civil War Desk Reference,* 631–34. See also Frank R. Freemon, *Gangrene and Glory: Medical Care during the American Civil War* (Madison, N.J.: Fairleigh Dickinson University Press, 1998).

[42]*Hospital Sketches,* 69. Wagner et al., *Library of Congress Civil War Desk Reference,* 624; McPherson, *Battle Cry of Freedom,* 484–89.

[43]*Hospital Sketches,* 69, 70. Georgeanna Woolsey, "How I Came to Be a Nurse," *Spirit of the Fair* (New York: New York Metropolitan Sanitary Fair, 1864), 136–37.

[44]For more graphic descriptions, see, for instance, Sophronia E. Bucklin, *In Hospital and Camp: A Woman's Record of Thrilling Incidents among the Wounded in the Late War* (Philadelphia, John E. Potter, 1869). *Hospital Sketches,* 70. Cornelia Hancock, *The South after Gettysburg,* ed. Henrietta Shatton Jaquette (New York: Crowell, 1956), 136–38.

[45]On Civil War medicine, see George Worthington Adams, *Doctors in Blue: The Medical History of the Union Army in the Civil War* (1952; reprint, New York: Collier, 1961); Stewart Brooks, *Civil War Medicine* (Springfield, Ill.: Charles C. Thomas, 1966); Paul E. Steiner, *Disease in the Civil War: Natural Biological Warfare in 1861–1865* (Springfield, Ill.: Charles C. Thomas, 1968); and Wagner et al., *Library of Congress Civil War Desk Reference,* 623–64.

[46]Wagner et al., *Library of Congress Civil War Desk Reference,* 627, 623; McPherson, *Battle Cry of Freedom,* 486.

[47]*Hospital Sketches,* 78, 116.

[48]Jane Stuart Woolsey, *Hospital Days: Reminiscence of a Civil War Nurse* (1868; reprint, Roseville, Minn.: Edinborough Press, 1996), 23.

[49]Woolsey, *Hospital Days,* 22.

[50]*Hospital Sketches,* 84. Wagner et al., *Library of Congress Civil War Desk Reference,* 624.

[51] Schultz, " 'Are We Not All Soldiers?' " 44.

[52] Emily Elizabeth Parsons, *Civil War Nursing: Memoir of Emily Elizabeth Parsons* (1880; reprint, New York: Garland, 1984), 18–21.

[53] Georgeanna Woolsey, "How I Came to Be a Nurse.—No. IV," *Spirit of the Fair,* April 16, 1864, 125.

[54] On friction between nurses and doctors, see Leonard, *Yankee Women;* and Ann Douglas Wood, "The War within a War: Women Nurses in the Union Army," *Civil War History* 18 (Sept. 1972): 191–212. *Hospital Sketches,* 117.

[55] Brinton quoted in Freemon, *Gangrene and Glory,* 54. *Hospital Sketches,* 77.

[56] *Hospital Sketches,* 87; Parsons, *Civil War Nursing,* 51. On "Mother" Bickerdyke, see Nina Brown Baker, *Cyclone in Calico: The Story of Mary Ann Bickerdyke* (Boston: Little, Brown, 1952).

[57] Ropes, *Civil War Nurse,* 121.

[58] Ropes, *Civil War Nurse,* 121. Bronson Alcott, *The Journals of Bronson Alcott,* ed. Odell Shepard (Boston: Little, Brown, 1938), 353. Bronson Alcott, *The Letters of A. Bronson Alcott,* ed. Richard L. Herrnstadt (Ames: Iowa State University Press, 1969), 333. *Journals,* 116. *Journals of Bronson Alcott,* 353. Ropes, *Civil War Nurse,* 124. *Journals,* 116. *Letters of A. Bronson Alcott,* 332, 336.

[59] *Journals of Bronson Alcott,* 352. *Journals,* 118.

[60] *Journals,* 118, 119. *American Publishers' Circular and Literary Gazette,* September 1, 1863, 346.

[61] *Journals,* 130.

[62] *Journals,* 119, 124.

[63] *Letters,* 86, 87. On women's self-deprecatory behavior within the literary marketplace of mid-nineteenth-century America, see Kelley, *Private Woman, Public Stage Journals,* 122.

[64] *Journals of Bronson Alcott,* 357. *Letters,* 88. *Journals,* 120. See the *Commonwealth* of October 2, 1863. *Journals,* 122.

[65] *Letters,* 85. "The Brothers" appeared in the November 1863 *Atlantic Monthly.* In December, she published *On Picket Duty, and Other Tales,* with James Redpath. The following year, she published several more pieces of war fiction, including "A Hospital Christmas" in the *Commonwealth* on January 8 and 15, 1864; a sketch called "The Hospital Lamp" in the February 24 and 25 issues of the *Daily Morning Drum-Beat,* a publication of the Brooklyn Sanitary Fair; "Love and Loyalty" in the *United States Service Magazine* between July and December 1864; and a children's war story called "Nelly's Hospital" in the April 1865 *Our Young Folks.* Alcott also continued to publish her "potboilers" during this period.

[66] *Journals,* 121.

[67] *Journals,* 127.

[68] The phrase "Sentimental Love Religion" is used by Barton Levi St. Armand in *Emily Dickinson and Her Culture: The Soul's Society* (New York: Cambridge University Press, 1984). On sentimentalism, see also Jane Tompkins, *Sensational Designs: The Cultural Work of American Fiction, 1790–1860* (New York: Oxford University Press, 1985); and Karen Halttunen, *Confidence Men and Painted Women: A Study of Middle-Class Culture in America, 1830–1870* (New Haven, Conn.: Yale University Press, 1982). On the ideology of domesticity, see especially Cott, *The Bonds of Womanhood.*

[69] See Chapter 17 of *Huck Finn* for Mark Twain's merciless skewering of mid-nineteenth-century sentimental culture. *Hospital Sketches,* 73, 118, 80, 75.

[70] *Hospital Sketches,* 113. *Letters,* 84, 97–98.

[71] *Hospital Sketches,* 87–88.

[72] *Hospital Sketches,* 53, 54, 55

[73] On the question of women's public role, see especially Mary Ryan, *Women in Public: Between Banners and Ballots, 1825–1880* (Baltimore: Johns Hopkins University Press, 1990). *Hospital Sketches,* 62.

[74]*Hospital Sketches,* 58, 59. On the quest for women's rights in the mid-nineteenth century, see especially Ellen DuBois, *Feminism and Suffrage* (Ithaca, N.Y.: Cornell University Press, 1978).

[75]*Hospital Sketches,* 71, 72.

[76]Fahs, *The Imagined Civil War,* 103–5.

[77]*Hospital Sketches,* 80, 71, 72.

[78]Oliver Wendell Holmes, "The Poetry of the War," unpublished 1865 lecture, Huntington Library, San Marino, California.

[79]Bell Irvin Wiley, *The Life of Billy Yank: The Common Soldier of the Union* (Indianapolis: Bobbs-Merrill, 1951; reprint, Baton Rouge: Louisiana State University Press, 1978), 299, 303; James M. McPherson, *Ordeal by Fire: The Civil War and Reconstruction,* rev. ed. (New York: McGraw-Hill, 1992), 355. "Nearly two-fifths of the soldiers were 21 or younger at the time of enlistment," according to McPherson. But of course, this also means that a majority of soldiers were not "boys."

[80]*Hospital Sketches,* 86–87.

[81]*Hospital Sketches,* 86, 88.

[82]*Hospital Sketches,* 89, 87.

[83]Ropes, *Civil War Nurse,* 117, 118.

[84]Ropes, *Civil War Nurse,* 118.

[85]On ideas and practices concerning death in mid-nineteenth-century America, see Fahs, *The Imagined Civil War,* 93–119; Drew Gilpin Faust, "The Civil War Soldier and the Art of Dying," *Journal of Southern History* 67 (2001): 3–38; and Gary Laderman, *The Sacred Remains: American Attitudes toward Death, 1799–1883* (New Haven, Conn.: Yale University Press, 1996).

[86]*Hospital Sketches,* 108, 77.

[87]*Hospital Sketches,* 92.

[88]Ropes, *Civil War Nurse,* 108.

[89]On the employment of African American and working-class women in hospitals, see especially Schultz, "'Are We Not All Soldiers?'" *Hospital Sketches,* 70, 105, 96.

[90]*Hospital Sketches,* 106, 105.

[91]The phrase "romantic racialism" is George Fredrickson's. George M. Fredrickson, *The Inner Civil War: Northern Intellectuals and the Crisis of the Union* (New York: Harper & Row, 1965). *Hospital Sketches,* 104, 67, 70, 106, 105.

[92]*Hospital Sketches,* 70, 73, 72.

[93]*Hospital Sketches,* 92. My thanks to Pat Kelly for his insights on wartime masculinity.

[94]Ropes, *Civil War Nurse,* 58. See also p. 74 for Ropes's claim that privates "were really the heroes of the war." *Notes of Hospital Life from November, 1861 to August, 1863* (Philadelphia: J. B. Lippincott, 1864), xii, dedication page.

[95]A. S. Hooker, "Hospital Heroes," *Frank Leslie's Illustrated Newspaper,* October 3, 1863, 21; Mrs. H. [Anna Morris Ellis Holstein], *Three Years in Field Hospitals of the Army of the Potomac* (Philadelphia: J. B. Lippincott, 1867), 47; William Howell Reed, *Hospital Life in the Army of the Potomac* (1866; reprint, Boston: William Howell Reed, 1891).

[96]*Hospital Sketches,* 72, 84.

[97]Walt Whitman to James Redpath, October 21, 1863, Whitman, *Collected Writings of Walt Whitman: The Correspondence,* Vol. 1 (New York: New York University Press, 1961), 171–72.

[98]Accounts by women include *Notes of Hospital Life;* Bucklin, *In Hospital and Camp;* Mrs. A. H. Hoge, *The Boys in Blue; Or, Heroes of the "Rank and File"* (New York: E. B. Treat, 1867); Amanda Akin Stearns, *The Lady Nurse of Ward E* (New York: Baker and Taylor, 1909); Annie Wittenmyer, *Under the Guns: A Woman's Reminiscences of the Civil War* (Boston: E. B. Stillings, 1895); Woolsey, *Hospital Days;* and Katherine Prescott Wormeley, *The Other Side of the War with the Army of the Potomac* (Boston: Ticknor, 1889). Stearns, *The Lady Nurse of Ward E,* 102.

The title page of the original edition of *Hospital Sketches*. The epigraph refers to the disreputable nurse Sairey Gamp, one of Charles Dickens's greatest comic inventions and a character in his 1844 *Martin Chuzzlewit*. Dickens was Alcott's favorite author, and references to his works abound in *Hospital Sketches*.

# HOSPITAL SKETCHES.

BY

## L. M. ALCOTT.

"Which, naming no names, no offence could be took."—*Sairy Gamp.*

---

BOSTON:

JAMES REDPATH, Publisher,

221 WASHINGTON STREET.

1863.

## PUBLISHER'S ADVERTISEMENT.

A considerable portion of this volume was published in successive numbers of *The Commonwealth*, newspaper, of Boston. The sudden popularity the Sketches won from the general public, and the praise they received from literary men of distinguished ability, are sufficient reasons,—were any needed, —for their re-publication, thus revised and enlarged, in this more convenient and permanent form. As, besides paying the Author the usual copyright, the publisher has resolved to devote at least five cents for every copy sold to the support of orphans made fatherless or homeless by the war, no reproduction of any part of the contents now first printed in these pages, will be permitted in any journal. Should the sale of the little book be large, the orphans' percentage will be doubled.

BOSTON, *August*, 1863.

The "Publisher's Advertisement" from the original edition of *Hospital Sketches.*

# PART TWO

# Hospital Sketches

*These Sketches
are respectfully dedicated
to her friend
Miss Hannah Stevenson,
by
L. M. A.*

## CHAPTER I. OBTAINING SUPPLIES

"I want something to do."

This remark being addressed to the world in general, no one in particular felt it their duty to reply; so I repeated it to the smaller world about me, received the following suggestions, and settled the matter by answering my own inquiry, as people are apt to do when very much in earnest.

"Write a book," quoth the author of my being.

"Don't know enough, sir. First live, then write."

"Try teaching again," suggested my mother.

"No thank you, ma'am, ten years of that is enough."

"Take a husband like my Darby, and fulfill your mission," said sister Joan, home on a visit.

"Can't afford expensive luxuries, Mrs. Coobiddy."

"Turn actress, and immortalize your name," said sister Vashti, striking an attitude.

"I won't."

"Go nurse the soldiers," said my young brother, Tom, panting for "the tented field."

"I will!"

So far, very good. Here was the will—now for the way. At first sight not a foot of it appeared, but that didn't matter, for the Periwinkles are a hopeful race; their crest is an anchor, with three cock-a-doodles crowing atop. They all wear rose-colored spectacles, and are lineal descendants of the inventor of aerial architecture. An hour's conversation on the subject set the whole family in a blaze of enthusiasm. A model hospital was erected, and each member had accepted an honorable post therein. The paternal P. was chaplain, the maternal R. was matron, and all the youthful P.s filled the pod of futurity with achievements whose brilliancy eclipsed the glories of the present and the past. Arriving at this satisfactory conclusion, the meeting adjourned, and the fact that Miss Tribulation was available as army nurse went abroad on the wings of the wind.

In a few days a townswoman heard of my desire, approved of it, and brought about an interview with one of the sisterhood which I wished to join, who was at home on a furlough, and able and willing to satisfy all inquiries. A morning chat with Miss General S.[1]—we hear no end of Mrs. Generals, why not a Miss?—produced three results: I felt that I could do the work, was offered a place, and accepted it, promising not to desert, but stand ready to march on Washington at an hour's notice.

A few days were necessary for the letter containing my request and recommendation to reach headquarters, and another, containing my commission, to return; therefore no time was to be lost; and heartily thanking my pair of friends, I tore home through the December slush as if the rebels were after me, and like many another recruit, burst in upon my family with the announcement—

"I've enlisted!"

An impressive silence followed. Tom, the irrepressible, broke it with a slap on the shoulder and the graceful compliment—

"Old Trib, you're a trump!"

"Thank you; then I'll *take* something:" which I did, in the shape of dinner, reeling off my news at the rate of three dozen words to a mouthful; and as every one else talked equally fast, and all together, the scene was most inspiring.

[1]*Miss General S.:* Alcott refers to Hannah Stevenson, a Boston reformer who had been a nurse in Washington and who helped Alcott find her position as a nurse.

As boys going to sea immediately become nautical in speech, walk as if they already had their "sea legs" on, and shiver their timbers on all possible occasions, so I turned military at once, called my dinner my rations, saluted all new comers, and ordered a dress parade that very afternoon. Having reviewed every rag I possessed, I detailed some for picket duty while airing over the fence; some to the sanitary influences of the wash-tub; others to mount guard in the trunk; while the weak and wounded went to the Work-basket Hospital, to be made ready for active service again. To this squad I devoted myself for a week; but all was done, and I had time to get powerfully impatient before the letter came. It did arrive however, and brought a disappointment along with its good will and friendliness, for it told me that the place in the Armory Hospital that I supposed I was to take, was already filled, and a much less desirable one at Hurly-burly House[2] was offered instead.

"That's just your luck, Trib. I'll tote your trunk up garret for you again; for of course you won't go," Tom remarked, with the disdainful pity which small boys affect when they get into their teens. I was wavering in my secret soul, but that settled the matter, and I crushed him on the spot with martial brevity —

"It is now one; I shall march at six."

I have a confused recollection of spending the afternoon in pervading the house like an executive whirlwind, with my family swarming after me, all working, talking, prophesying and lamenting, while I packed my "go-abroady" possessions, tumbled the rest into two big boxes, danced on the lids till they shut, and gave them in charge, with the direction, —

"If I never come back, make a bonfire of them."

Then I choked down a cup of tea, generously salted instead of sugared, by some agitated relative, shouldered my knapsack — it was only a traveling bag, but do let me preserve the unities — hugged my family three times all round without a vestige of unmanly emotion, till a certain dear old lady broke down upon my neck, with a despairing sort of wail —

"Oh, my dear, my dear, how can I let you go?"

"I'll stay if you say so, mother."

"But I don't; go, and the Lord will take care of you."

Much of the Roman matron's courage had gone into the Yankee

---

[2]*Armory Hospital, Hurly-burly House:* The Armory Square Hospital, built in 1862, was a large, well-run institution. *Hurly-burly House* refers to the much less well run Union Hotel Hospital.

matron's composition, and, in spite of her tears, she would have sent ten sons to the war, had she possessed them, as freely as she sent one daughter, smiling and flapping on the door-step till I vanished, though the eyes that followed me were very dim, and the handkerchief she waved was very wet.

My transit from The Gables to the village depot was a funny mixture of good wishes and good byes, mud-puddles and shopping. A December twilight is not the most cheering time to enter upon a somewhat perilous enterprise, and, but for the presence of Vashti and neighbor Thorn, I fear that I might have added a drop of the briny to the native moisture of—

"The town I left behind me;"[3]

though I'd no thought of giving out: oh, bless you, no! When the engine screeched "Here we are," I clutched my escort in a fervent embrace, and skipped into the car with as blithe a farewell as if going on a bridal tour—though I believe brides don't usually wear cavernous black bonnets and fuzzy brown coats, with a hair-brush, a pair of rubbers, two books, and a bag of ginger-bread distorting the pockets of the same. If I thought that any one would believe it, I'd boldly state that I slept from C. to B., which would simplify matters immensely; but as I know they wouldn't, I'll confess that the head under the funereal coal-hod fermented with all manner of high thoughts and heroic purposes "to do or die,"—perhaps both; and the heart under the fuzzy brown coat felt very tender with the memory of the dear old lady, probably sobbing over her army socks and the loss of her topsy-turvy Trib. At this juncture I took the veil, and what I did behind it is nobody's business; but I maintain that the soldier who cries when his mother says "Good bye," is the boy to fight best, and die bravest, when the time comes, or go back to her better than he went.

Till nine o'clock I trotted about the city streets, doing those last errands which no woman would even go to heaven without attempting, if she could. Then I went to my usual refuge, and, fully intending to keep awake, as a sort of vigil appropriate to the occasion, fell fast asleep and dreamed propitious dreams till my rosy-faced cousin waked me with a kiss.

[3] Alcott makes a gentle joke of the title of one of the most popular songs of the Civil War, "The Girl I Left Behind Me," an old Irish tune that had also been popular during the Revolutionary War.

A bright day smiled upon my enterprise, and at ten I reported myself to my General, received last instructions and no end of the sympathetic encouragement which women give, in look, touch, and tone more effectually than in words. The next step was to get a free pass to Washington, for I'd no desire to waste my substance on railroad companies when "the boys" needed even a spinster's mite. A friend of mine had procured such a pass, and I was bent on doing likewise, though I had to face the president of the railroad to accomplish it. I'm a bashful individual, though I can't get any one to believe it; so it cost me a great effort to poke about the Worcester depot till the right door appeared, then walk into a room containing several gentlemen, and blunder out my request in a high state of stammer and blush. Nothing could have been more courteous than this dreaded President, but it was evident that I had made as absurd a demand as if I had asked for the nose off his respectable face. He referred me to the Governor at the State House, and I backed out, leaving him no doubt to regret that such mild maniacs were left at large. Here was a Scylla and Charybdis[4] business: as if a President wasn't trying enough, without the Governor of Massachusetts and the hub of the hub piled on top of that. "I never can do it," thought I. "Tom will hoot at you if you don't," whispered the inconvenient little voice that is always goading people to the performance of disagreeable duties, and always appeals to the most effective agent to produce the proper result. The idea of allowing any boy that ever wore a felt basin and a shoddy jacket with a microscopic tail, to crow over me, was preposterous, so giving myself a mental slap for such faint-heartedness, I streamed away across the Common, wondering if I ought to say "your Honor," or simply "Sir," and decided upon the latter, fortifying myself with recollections of an evening in a charming green library, where I beheld the Governor placidly consuming oysters, and laughing as if Massachusetts was a myth, and he had no heavier burden on his shoulders than his host's handsome hands.

Like an energetic fly in a very large cobweb, I struggled through the State House, getting into all the wrong rooms and none of the right, till I turned desperate, and went into one, resolving not to come out till I'd made somebody hear and answer me. I suspect that of all the wrong places I had blundered into, this was the most so. But I didn't care; and, though the apartment was full of soldiers, surgeons,

---

[4] *Scylla and Charybdis:* In Greek mythology, the sea monsters Scylla and Charybdis were twin dangers facing sailors. Avoidance of either meant exposure to the other.

starers, and spittoons, I cornered a perfectly incapable person, and proceeded to pump for information with the following result:

"Was the Governor anywhere about?"

No, he wasn't.

"Could he tell me where to look?"

No, he couldn't.

"Did he know anything about free passes?"

No, he didn't.

"Was there any one there of whom I could inquire?"

Not a person.

"Did he know of any place where information could be obtained?"

Not a place.

"Could he throw the smallest gleam of light upon the matter, in any way?"

Not a ray.

I am naturally irascible, and if I could have shaken this negative gentleman vigorously, the relief would have been immense. The prejudices of society forbidding this mode of redress, I merely glowered at him; and, before my wrath found vent in words, my General appeared, having seen me from an opposite window, and come to know what I was about. At her command the languid gentleman woke up, and troubled himself to remember that Major or Sergeant or something Mc K. knew all about the tickets, and his office was in Milk Street. I perked up instanter, and then, as if the exertion was too much for him, what did this animated wet blanket do but add—

"I think Mc K. may have left Milk Street, now, and I don't know where he has gone."

"Never mind; the new comers will know where he has moved to, my dear, so don't be discouraged; and if you don't succeed, come to me, and we will see what to do next," said my General.

I blessed her in a fervent manner and a cool hall, fluttered round the corner, and bore down upon Milk street, bent on discovering Mc K. if such a being was to be found. He wasn't, and the ignorance of the neighborhood was really pitiable. Nobody knew anything, and after tumbling over bundles of leather, bumping against big boxes, being nearly annihilated by descending bales, and sworn at by aggravated truckmen, I finally elicited the advice to look for Mc K. in Haymarket Square. Who my informant was I've really forgotten; for, having hailed several busy gentlemen, some one of them fabricated this delusive quietus for the perturbed spirit, who instantly departed to the sequestered locality he named. If I had been in search of the

Koh-i-noor diamond I should have been as likely to find it there as any vestige of Mc K. I stared at signs, inquired in shops, invaded an eating house, visited the recruiting tent in the middle of the Square, made myself a nuisance generally, and accumulated mud enough to retard another Nile. All in vain: and I mournfully turned my face toward the General's, feeling that I should be forced to enrich the railroad company after all; when, suddenly, I beheld that admirable young man, brother-in-law Darby Coobiddy, Esq. I arrested him with a burst of news, and wants, and woes, which caused his manly countenance to lose its usual repose.

"Oh, my dear boy, I'm going to Washington at five, and I can't find the free ticket man, and there won't be time to see Joan, and I'm so tired and cross I don't know what to do; and will you help me, like a cherub as you are?"

"Oh, yes, of course. I know a fellow who will set us right," responded Darby, mildly excited, and darting into some kind of an office, held counsel with an invisible angel, who sent him out radiant. "All serene. I've got him. I'll see you through the business, and then get Joan from the Dove Cote in time to see you off."

I'm a woman's rights woman,[5] and if any man had offered help in the morning, I should have condescendingly refused it, sure that I could do everything as well, if not better, myself. My strong-mindedness had rather abated since then, and I was now quite ready to be a "timid trembler," if necessary. Dear me! how easily Darby did it all: he just asked one question, received an answer, tucked me under his arm, and in ten minutes I stood in the presence of Mc K., the Desired.

"Now my troubles are over," thought I, and as usual was direfully mistaken.

"You will have to get a pass from Dr. H., in Temple Place, before I can give you a pass, madam," answered Mc K., as blandly as if he wasn't carrying desolation to my soul. Oh, indeed! why didn't he send me to Dorchester Heights, India Wharf, or Bunker Hill Monument, and done with it? Here I was, after a morning's tramp, down in some place about Dock Square, and was told to step to Temple Place. Nor was that all; he might as well have asked me to catch a humming-bird, toast a salamander, or call on the man in the moon, as find a Doctor at

[5]Committed to the cause of woman's rights throughout her adult life, after the Civil War Alcott became an activist for woman's suffrage as well. In 1875, she attended the Women's Congress in Syracuse, New York; she also contributed to Lucy Stone's *Woman's Journal.* In her fiction, she repeatedly explored the question of women's limited work options; her 1873 novel, *Work,* was a sustained exploration of this theme.

home at the busiest hour of the day. It was a blow; but weariness had extinguished enthusiasm, and resignation clothed me as a garment. I sent Darby for Joan, and doggedly paddled off, feeling that mud was my native element, and quite sure that the evening papers would announce the appearance of the Wandering Jew, in feminine habiliments.

"Is Dr. H. in?"

"No, mum, he aint."

Of course he wasn't; I knew that before I asked: and, considering it all in the light of a hollow mockery, added:

"When will he probably return?"

If the damsel had said, "ten to-night," I should have felt a grim satisfaction, in the fulfillment of my own dark prophecy; but she said, "At two, mum;" and I felt it a personal insult.

"I'll call, then. Tell him my business is important:" with which mysteriously delivered message I departed, hoping that I left her consumed with curiosity; for mud rendered me an object of interest.

By way of resting myself, I crossed the Common, for the third time, bespoke the carriage, got some lunch, packed my purchases, smoothed my plumage, and was back again, as the clock struck two. The Doctor hadn't come yet; and I was morally certain that he would not, till, having waited till the last minute, I was driven to buy a ticket, and, five minutes after the irrevocable deed was done, he would be at my service, with all manner of helpful documents and directions. Everything goes by contraries with me; so, having made up my mind to be disappointed, of course I wasn't; for, presently, in walked Dr. H., and no sooner had he heard my errand, and glanced at my credentials, than he said, with the most engaging readiness:

"I will give you the order, with pleasure, madam."

Words cannot express how soothing and delightful it was to find, at last, somebody who could do what I wanted, without sending me from Dan to Beersheba,[6] for a dozen other bodies to do something else first. Peace descended, like oil, upon the ruffled waters of my being, as I sat listening to the busy scratch of his pen; and, when he turned about, giving me not only the order, but a paper of directions wherewith to smooth away all difficulties between Boston and Washington, I felt as did poor Christian when the Evangelist gave him the scroll,[7] on

[6]*Dan to Beersheba:* A familiar saying from the Bible to express the extent of territory in Israel, from the northernmost city of Dan to the southernmost city of Beersheba.

[7]Alcott refers to the first chapter of John Bunyan's *Pilgrim's Progress,* a popular text for children in mid-nineteenth-century America.

the safe side of the Slough of Despond. I've no doubt many dismal nurses have inflicted themselves upon the worthy gentleman since then; but I am sure none have been more kindly helped, or are more grateful, than T. P.; for that short interview added another to the many pleasant associations that already surround his name.

Feeling myself no longer a "Martha Struggles," but a comfortable young woman, with plain sailing before her, and the worst of the voyage well over, I once more presented myself to the valuable Mc K. The order was read, and certain printed papers, necessary to be filled out, were given a young gentleman—no, I prefer to say Boy, with a scornful emphasis upon the word, as the only means of revenge now left me. This BOY, instead of doing his duty with the diligence so charming in the young, loitered and lounged, in a manner which proved his education to have been sadly neglected in the—

"How doth the little busy bee,"[8]

direction. He stared at me, gaped out of the window, ate peanuts, and gossiped with his neighbors—Boys, like himself, and all penned in a row, like colts at a Cattle Show. I don't imagine he knew the anguish he was inflicting; for it was nearly three, the train left at five, and I had my ticket to get, my dinner to eat, my blessed sister to see, and the depot to reach, if I didn't die of apoplexy. Meanwhile, Patience certainly had her perfect work that day, and I hope she enjoyed the job more than I did. Having waited some twenty minutes, it pleased this reprehensible Boy to make various marks and blots on my documents, toss them to a venerable creature of sixteen, who delivered them to me with such paternal directions, that it only needed a pat on the head and an encouraging—"Now run home to your Ma, little girl, and mind the crossings, my dear," to make the illusion quite perfect.

Why I was sent to a steamboat office for car tickets is not for me to say, though I went as meekly as I should have gone to the Probate Court, if sent. A fat, easy gentleman gave me several bits of paper, with coupons attached, with a warning not to separate them, which instantly inspired me with a yearning to pluck them apart, and see what came of it. But, remembering through what fear and tribulation I had obtained them, I curbed Satan's promptings and, clutching my prize, as if it were my pass to the Elysian Fields,[9] I hurried home.

---

[8]Here Alcott quotes from a popular didactic children's poem, "Against Idleness and Mischief," by Isaac Watts (1674–1748). The complete verse from which she quotes reads, "How doth the little busy Bee/Improve each shining Hour,/And gather honey all the day/From every opening Flower!"

[9]*Elysian Fields:* In Greek mythology, paradise.

Dinner was rapidly consumed; Joan enlightened, comforted, and kissed; the dearest of apple-faced cousins hugged; the kindest of apple-faced cousins' fathers subjected to the same process; and I mounted the ambulance, baggage-wagon, or anything you please but hack, and drove away, too tired to feel excited, sorry, or glad.

## CHAPTER II. A FORWARD MOVEMENT

As travellers like to give their own impressions of a journey, though every inch of the way may have been described a half a dozen times before, I add some of the notes made by the way, hoping that they will amuse the reader, and convince the skeptical that such a being as Nurse Periwinkle does exist, that she really did go to Washington, and that these Sketches are not romance.

*New York Train—Seven P. M.*—Spinning along to take the boat at New London. Very comfortable; munch gingerbread, and Mrs. C.'s fine pear, which deserves honorable mention, because my first loneliness was comforted by it, and pleasant recollections of both kindly sender and bearer. Look much at Dr. H.'s paper of directions—put my tickets in every conceivable place, that they may be get-at-able, and finish by losing them entirely. Suffer agonies till a compassionate neighbor pokes them out of a crack with his pen-knife. Put them in the inmost corner of my purse, that in the deepest recesses of my pocket, pile a collection of miscellaneous articles atop, and pin up the whole. Just get composed, feeling that I've done my best to keep them safely, when the Conductor appears, and I'm forced to rout them all out again, exposing my precautions, and getting into a flutter at keeping the man waiting. Finally, fasten them on the seat before me, and keep one eye steadily upon the yellow torments, till I forget all about them, in chat with the gentleman who shares my seat. Having heard complaints of the absurd way in which American women become images of petrified propriety, if addressed by strangers, when traveling alone, the inborn perversity of my nature causes me to assume an entirely opposite style of deportment; and, finding my companion hails from Little Athens, is acquainted with several of my three hundred and sixty-five cousins, and in every way a respectable and respectful member of society, I put my bashfulness in my pocket, and plunge into a long conversation on the war, the weather, music, Carlyle, skating, genius, hoops, and the immortality of the soul.

*Ten, P. M.*—Very sleepy. Nothing to be seen outside, but darkness made visible; nothing inside but every variety of bunch into which the human form can be twisted, rolled, or "massed," as Miss Prescott says of her jewels. Every man's legs sprawl drowsily, every woman's head (but mine,) nods, till it finally settles on somebody's shoulder, a new proof of the truth of the everlasting oak and vine simile;[10] children fret; lovers whisper; old folks snore, and somebody privately imbibes brandy, when the lamps go out. The penetrating perfume rouses the multitude, causing some to start up, like war horses at the smell of powder. When the lamps are relighted, every one laughs, sniffs, and looks inquiringly at his neighbor—every one but a stout gentleman, who, with well-gloved hands folded upon his broad-cloth rotundity, sleeps on impressively. Had he been innocent, he would have waked up; for, to slumber in that babe-like manner, with a car full of giggling, staring, sniffing humanity, was simply preposterous. Public suspicion was down upon him at once. I doubt if the appearance of a fat black bottle with a label would have settled the matter more effectually than did the over dignified and profound repose of this short-sighted being. His moral neck-cloth, virtuous boots, and pious attitude availed him nothing, and it was well he kept his eyes shut, for "Humbug!" twinkled at him from every window-pane, brass nail and human eye around him.

*Eleven, P. M.*—In the boat "City of Boston," escorted thither by my car acquaintance, and deposited in the cabin. Trying to look as if the greater portion of my life had been passed on board boats, but painfully conscious that I don't know the first thing; so sit bolt upright, and stare about me till I hear one lady say to another—"We must secure our berths at once;" whereupon I dart at one, and, while leisurely taking off my cloak, wait to discover what the second move may be. Several ladies draw the curtains that hang in a semi-circle before each nest—instantly I whisk mine smartly together, and then peep out to see what next. Gradually, on hooks above the blue and yellow drapery, appear the coats and bonnets of my neighbors, while their boots and shoes, in every imaginable attitude, assert themselves below, as if their owners had committed suicide in a body. A violent creaking, scrambling, and fussing, causes the fact that people are going regularly to bed to dawn upon my mind. Of course they are! and so am I—but pause at the seventh pin, remembering that, as I was born to be drowned, an eligible opportunity now presents itself; and,

---

[10]Comparisons of men to "sturdy oaks" and women to "clinging vines" were common in mid-nineteenth-century sentimental culture.

having twice escaped a watery grave, the third immersion will certainly extinguish my vital spark. The boat is new, but if it ever intends to blow up, spring a leak, catch afire, or be run into, it will do the deed tonight, because I'm here to fulfill my destiny. With tragic calmness I resign myself, replace my pins, lash my purse and papers together, with my handkerchief, examine the saving circumference of my hoop, and look about me for any means of deliverance when the moist moment shall arrive; for I've no intention of folding my hands and bubbling to death without an energetic splashing first. Barrels, hen-coops, portable settees, and life-preservers do not adorn the cabin, as they should; and, roving wildly to and fro, my eye sees no ray of hope till it falls upon a plump old lady, devoutly reading in the cabin Bible, and a voluminous night-cap. I remember that, at the swimming school, fat girls always floated best, and in an instant my plan is laid. At the first alarm I firmly attach myself to the plump lady, and cling to her through fire and water; for I feel that my old enemy, the cramp, will seize me by the foot, if I attempt to swim; and, though I can hardly expect to reach Jersey City with myself and my baggage in as good condition as I hoped, I might manage to get picked up by holding to my fat friend; if not it will be a comfort to feel that I've made an effort and shall die in good society. Poor dear woman! how little she dreamed, as she read and rocked, with her cap in a high state of starch, and her feet comfortably cooking at the register, what fell designs were hovering about her, and how intently a small but determined eye watched her, till it suddenly closed.

Sleep got the better of fear to such an extent that my boots appeared to gape, and my bonnet nodded on its peg, before I gave in. Having piled my cloak, bag, rubbers, books and umbrella on the lower shelf, I drowsily swarmed onto the upper one, tumbling down a few times, and excoriating the knobby portions of my frame in the act. A very brief nap on the upper roost was enough to set me gasping as if a dozen feather beds and the whole boat were laid over me. Out I turned; and, after a series of convulsions, which caused my neighbor to ask if I wanted the stewardess, I managed to get my luggage up and myself down. But even in the lower berth, my rest was not unbroken, for various articles kept dropping off the little shelf at the bottom of the bed, and every time I flew up, thinking my hour had come, I bumped my head severely against the little shelf at the top, evidently put there for that express purpose. At last, after listening to the swash of the waves outside, wondering if the machinery usually creaked in that way, and watching a knot-hole in the side of my berth, sure that death would creep in there as soon as I took my eye from it, I dropped asleep, and dreamed of muffins.

*Five, A. M.*—On deck, trying to wake up and enjoy an east wind and a morning fog, and a twilight sort of view of something on the shore. Rapidly achieve my purpose, and do enjoy every moment, as we go rushing through the Sound, with steamboats passing up and down, lights dancing on the shore, mist wreaths slowly furling off, and a pale pink sky above us, as the sun comes up.

*Seven, A. M.*—In the cars, at Jersey City. Much fuss with tickets, which one man scribbles over, another snips, and a third "makes note on." Partake of refreshment, in the gloom of a very large and dirty depot. Think that my sandwiches would be more relishing without so strong a flavor of napkin, and my gingerbread more easy of consumption if it had not been pulverized by being sat upon. People act as if early travelling didn't agree with them. Children scream and scamper; men smoke and growl; women shiver and fret; porters swear; great truck horses pace up and down with loads of baggage; and every one seems to get into the wrong car, and come tumbling out again. One man, with three children, a dog, a bird-cage, and several bundles, puts himself and his possessions into every possible place where a man, three children, dog, bird-cage and bundles could be got, and is satisfied with none of them. I follow their movements, with an interest that is really exhausting, and, as they vanish, hope for rest, but don't get it. A strong-minded woman, with a tumbler in her hand, and no cloak or shawl on, comes rushing through the car, talking loudly to a small porter, who lugs a folding bed after her, and looks as if life were a burden to him.

"You promised to have it ready. It is not ready. It must be a car with a water jar, the windows must be shut, the fire must be kept up, the blinds must be down. No, this won't do. I shall go through the whole train, and suit myself, for you promised to have it ready. It is not ready," &c., all through again, like a hand-organ. She haunted the cars, the depot, the office and baggage-room, with her bed, her tumbler, and her tongue, till the train started; and a sense of fervent gratitude filled my soul, when I found that she and her unknown invalid were not to share our car.

*Philadelphia.*—An old place, full of Dutch women, in "bellus top" bonnets, selling vegetables, in long, open markets. Every one seems to be scrubbing their white steps. All the houses look like tidy jails, with their outside shutters. Several have crape on the door-handles, and many have flags flying from roof or balcony. Few men appear, and the women seem to do the business, which, perhaps, accounts for its being so well done. Pass fine buildings, but don't know what they are. Would like to stop and see my native city; for, having left it at the tender age of two, my recollections are not vivid.

*Baltimore.* — A big, dirty, shippy, shiftless place, full of goats, geese, colored people, and coal, at least the part of it I see. Pass near the spot where the riot[11] took place, and feel as if I should enjoy throwing a stone at somebody, hard. Find a guard at the ferry, the depot, and here and there, along the road. A camp whitens one hill-side, and a cavalry training school, or whatever it should be called, is a very interesting sight, with quantities of horses and riders galloping, marching, leaping, and skirmishing, over all manner of break-neck places. A party of English people get in — the men, with sandy hair and red whiskers, all trimmed alike, to a hair; rough grey coats, very rosy, clean faces, and a fine, full way of speaking, which is particularly agreeable, after our slipshod American gabble. The two ladies wear funny velvet fur-trimmed hoods; are done up, like compact bundles, in tartan shawls; and look as if bent on seeing everything thoroughly. The devotion of one elderly John Bull[12] to his red-nosed spouse was really beautiful to behold. She was plain and cross, and fussy and stupid, but J. B., Esq., read no papers when she was awake, turned no cold shoulder when she wished to sleep, and cheerfully said, "Yes, me dear," to every wish or want the wife of his bosom expressed. I quite warmed to the excellent man, and asked a question or two, as the only means of expressing my good will. He answered very civilly, but evidently hadn't been used to being addressed by strange women in public conveyances; and Mrs. B. fixed her green eyes upon me, as if she thought me a forward huzzy, or whatever is good English for a presuming young woman. The pair left their friends before we reached Washington; and the last I saw of them was a vision of a large plaid lady, stalking grimly away, on the arm of a rosy, stout gentleman, loaded with rugs, bags, and books, but still devoted, still smiling, and waving a hearty "Fare ye well! We'll meet ye at Willard's on Chusday."

Soon after their departure we had an accident; for no long journey in America would be complete without one. A coupling iron broke; and, after leaving the last car behind us, we waited for it to come up,

[11]*the riot:* On April 19, 1861, as the Sixth Massachusetts Regiment passed through Baltimore on the way to Washington, it was attacked by a mob of Confederate sympathizers.

[12]*John Bull:* Just as Uncle Sam was a figure representing Americans in the nineteenth century, John Bull was a figure representing Englishmen.

which it did, with a crash that knocked every one forward on their faces, and caused several old ladies to screech dismally. Hats flew off, bonnets were flattened, the stove skipped, the lamps fell down, the water jar turned a somersault, and the wheel just over which I sat received some damage. Of course, it became necessary for all the men to get out, and stand about in everybody's way, while repairs were made; and for the women to wrestle their heads out of the windows, asking ninety-nine foolish questions to one sensible one. A few wise females seized this favorable moment to better their seats, well knowing that few men can face the wooden stare with which they regard the former possessors of the places they have invaded.

The country through which we passed did not seem so very unlike that which I had left, except that it was more level and less wintry. In summer time the wide fields would have shown me new sights, and the way-side hedges blossomed with new flowers; now, everything was sere and sodden, and a general air of shiftlessness prevailed, which would have caused a New England farmer much disgust, and a strong desire to "buckle to," and "right up" things. Dreary little houses, with chimneys built outside, with clay and rough sticks piled crosswise, as we used to build cob towers, stood in barren looking fields, with cow, pig, or mule lounging about the door. We often passed colored people, looking as if they had come out of a picture book, or off the stage, but not at all the sort of people I'd been accustomed to see at the North.

Way-side encampments made the fields and lanes gay with blue coats and the glitter of buttons. Military washes flapped and fluttered on the fences; pots were steaming in the open air; all sorts of tableaux seen through the openings of tents, and everywhere the boys threw up their caps and cut capers as we passed.

*Washington.* — It was dark when we arrived; and, but for the presence of another friendly gentleman, I should have yielded myself a helpless prey to the first overpowering hackman, who insisted that I wanted to go just where I didn't. Putting me into the conveyance I belonged in, my escort added to the obligation by pointing out the objects of interest which we passed in our long drive. Though I'd often been told that Washington was a spacious place, its visible magnitude quite took my break away, and of course I quoted Randolph's expression, "a city of magnificent distances," as I suppose every one does when they see it. The Capitol was so like the pictures that hang opposite the staring Father of his Country, in boarding-houses and hotels, that it did not impress me, except to recall the time when I was sure that Cinderella went to housekeeping in just such a place, after she had married the inflammable Prince; though, even at that early period, I had my doubts as to the wisdom of a match whose foundation was of glass.

The White House was lighted up, and carriages were rolling in and out of the great gate. I stared hard at the famous East Room, and would have liked a peep through the crack of the door. My old gentleman was indefatigable in his attentions, and I said "Splendid!" to everything he pointed out, though I suspect I often admired the wrong place, and missed the right. Pennsylvania Avenue, with its bustle, lights, music, and military, made me feel as if I'd crossed the water and landed somewhere in Carnival time. Coming to less noticeable parts of the city, my companion fell silent, and I meditated upon the perfection which Art had attained in America—having just passed a bronze statue of some hero, who looked like a black Methodist minister, in a cocked hat, above the waist, and a tipsy squire below; while his horse stood like an opera dancer, on one leg, in a high, but somewhat remarkable wind, which blew his mane one way and his massive tail the other.

"Hurly-burly House, ma'am!" called a voice, startling me from my reverie, as we stopped before a great pile of buildings, with a flag flying before it, sentinels at the door, and a very trying quantity of men lounging about. My heart beat rather faster than usual, and it suddenly struck me that I was very far from home; but I descended with dignity, wondering whether I should be stopped for want of a countersign, and forced to pass the night in the street. Marching boldly up the steps, I found that no form was necessary, for the men fell back, the guard touched their caps, a boy opened the door, and, as it closed behind me, I felt that I was fairly started, and Nurse Periwinkle's Mission was begun.

## CHAPTER III. A DAY

"They've come! they've come! hurry up, ladies—you're wanted."

"Who have come? the rebels?"

This sudden summons in the gray dawn was somewhat startling to a three days' nurse like myself, and, as the thundering knock came at our door, I sprang up in my bed, prepared

> "To gird my woman's form,
> And on the ramparts die,"

if necessary, but my room-mate took it more coolly, and, as she began a rapid toilet, answered my bewildered question,—

"Bless you, no child; it's the wounded from Fredericksburg;[13] forty ambulances are at the door, and we shall have our hands full in fifteen minutes."

"What shall we have to do?"

"Wash, dress, feed, warm and nurse them for the next three months, I dare say. Eighty beds are ready, and we were getting impatient for the men to come. Now you will begin to see hospital life in earnest, for you won't probably find time to sit down all day, and may think yourself fortunate if you get to bed by midnight. Come to me in the ball-room when you are ready; the worst cases are always carried there, and I shall need your help."

So saying, the energetic little woman twirled her hair into a button at the back of her head, in a "cleared for action" sort of style, and vanished, wrestling her way into a feminine kind of pea-jacket as she went.

I am free to confess that I had a realizing sense of the fact that my hospital bed was not a bed of roses just then, or the prospect before me one of unmingled rapture. My three days' experiences had begun with a death, and, owing to the defalcation of another nurse, a somewhat abrupt plunge into the superintendence of a ward containing forty beds, where I spent my shining hours washing faces, serving rations, giving medicine, and sitting in a very hard chair, with pneumonia on one side, diptheria on the other, five typhoids on the opposite, and a dozen dilapidated patriots, hopping, lying, and lounging about, all staring more or less at the new "nuss," who suffered untold agonies, but concealed them under as matronly an aspect as a spinster could assume, and blundered through her trying labors with a Spartan firmness, which I hope they appreciated, but am afraid they didn't. Having a taste for "ghastliness," I had rather longed for the wounded to arrive, for rheumatism wasn't heroic, neither was liver complaint, or measles; even fever had lost its charms since "bathing burning brows" had been used up in romances, real and ideal; but when I peeped into the dusky street lined with what I at first had innocently called market carts, now unloading their sad freight at our door, I recalled sundry reminiscences I had heard from nurses of longer standing, my ardor experienced a sudden chill, and I indulged in a most unpatriotic wish

[13] *Fredericksburg:* One of the major battles of the Civil War. It began on December 11, 1862. (See the introduction.)

that I was safe at home again, with a quiet day before me, and no necessity for being hustled up, as if I were a hen and had only to hop off my roost, give my plumage a peck, and be ready for action. A second bang at the door sent this recreant desire to the right about, as a little woolly head popped in, and Joey, (a six years' old contraband,[14]) announced—

"Miss Blank is jes' wild fer ye, and says fly round right away. They's comin' in, I tell yer, heaps on 'em—one was took out dead, and I see him,—ky! warn't he a goner!"

With which cheerful intelligence the imp scuttled away, singing like a blackbird, and I followed, feeling that Richard was *not* himself again,[15] and wouldn't be for a long time to come.

The first thing I met was a regiment of the vilest odors that ever assaulted the human nose, and took it by storm. Cologne, with its seven and seventy evil savors, was a posy-bed to it; and the worst of this affliction was, every one had assured me that it was a chronic weakness of all hospitals, and I must bear it. I did, armed with lavender water, with which I so besprinkled myself and premises, that, like my friend, Sairy, I was soon known among my patients as "the nurse with the bottle." Having been run over by three excited surgeons, bumped against by migratory coal-hods, water-pails, and small boys; nearly scalded by an avalanche of newly-filled tea-pots, and hopelessly entangled in a knot of colored sisters[16] coming to wash, I progressed by slow stages up stairs and down, till the main hall was reached, and I paused to take breath and a survey. There they were! "our brave boys," as the papers justly call them, for cowards could hardly have been so riddled with shot and shell, so torn and shattered, nor have borne suffering for which we have no name, with an uncomplaining fortitude, which made one glad to cherish each as a brother. In they

---

[14]*contraband:* By June 1861, slaves had begun the dramatic process of freeing themselves by entering Union lines in Virginia. At Fortress Monroe, General Benjamin Butler designated these former slaves "contraband" of war to prevent their being returned to their former owners. *Contrabands* quickly became a popular term in the North to describe these former slaves, but it should be noted that the term had racist overtones, as it continued to designate former slaves as a form of property.

[15]*Richard was* not *himself again:* A quotation from a version of Shakespeare's *Richard III* that was still popular in Alcott's lifetime; the actual quotation, however—"Richard is Himself again"—was not written by Shakespeare, but by a later author, Colley Cibber, who "improved" the play.

[16]*colored sisters:* African American women performed much of the hard labor in Washington hospitals during the war. Here we get only a glimpse of these women, who are often invisible in wartime accounts by whites.

came, some on stretchers, some in men's arms, some feebly stagger-
ing along propped on rude crutches, and one lay stark and still with
covered face, as a comrade gave his name to be recorded before they
carried him away to the dead house. All was hurry and confusion; the
hall was full of these wrecks of humanity, for the most exhausted
could not reach a bed till duly ticketed and registered; the walls were
lined with rows of such as could sit, the floor covered with the more
disabled, the steps and doorways filled with helpers and lookers on;
the sound of many feet and voices made that usually quiet hour as
noisy as noon; and, in the midst of it all, the matron's motherly face
brought more comfort to many a poor soul, than the cordial draughts
she administered, or the cheery words that welcomed all, making of
the hospital a home.

The sight of several stretchers, each with its legless, armless, or
desperately wounded occupant, entering my ward, admonished me
that I was there to work, not to wonder or weep; so I corked up my
feelings, and returned to the path of duty, which was rather "a hard
road to travel" just then. The house had been a hotel before hospitals
were needed, and many of the doors still bore their old names; some
not so inappropriate as might be imagined, for my ward was in truth a
*ball-room,* if gun-shot wounds could christen it. Forty beds were prepared, many already tenanted by tired men who fell down anywhere,
and drowsed till the smell of food roused them. Round the great stove
was gathered the dreariest group I ever saw—ragged, gaunt and pale,
mud to the knees, with bloody bandages untouched since put on days
before; many bundled up in blankets, coats being lost, or useless; and
all wearing that disheartened look which proclaimed defeat, more
plainly than any telegram of the Burnside blunder.[17] I pitied them so
much, I dared not speak to them, though, remembering all they had
been through since the route[18] at Fredericksburg, I yearned to serve
the dreariest of them all. Presently, Miss Blank tore me from my
refuge behind piles of one-sleeved shirts, odd socks, bandages and
lint; put basin, sponge, towels, and a block of brown soap into my
hands, with these appalling directions:

"Come, my dear, begin to wash as fast as you can. Tell them to take
off socks, coats and shirts; scrub them well, put on clean shirts, and
the attendants will finish them off, and lay them in bed."

---

[17]*Burnside blunder:* A reference to General Ambrose Burnside, who commanded
Union troops at the Battle of Fredericksburg.
[18]*route:* Alcott means "rout."

If she had requested me to shave them all, or dance a hornpipe on the stove funnel, I should have been less staggered; but to scrub some dozen lords of creation at a moment's notice, was really—really——. However, there was no time for nonsense, and, having resolved when I came to do everything I was bid, I drowned my scruples in my wash-bowl, clutched my soap manfully, and, assuming a business-like air, made a dab at the first dirty specimen I saw, bent on performing my task *vi et armis*[19] if necessary. I chanced to light on a withered old Irishman, wounded in the head, which caused that portion of his frame to be tastefully laid out like a garden, the bandages being the walks, his hair the shrubbery. He was so overpowered by the honor of having a lady wash him, as he expressed it, that he did nothing but roll up his eyes, and bless me, in an irresistible style which was too much for my sense of the ludicrous; so we laughed together, and when I knelt down to take off his shoes, he "flopped" also and wouldn't hear of my touching "them dirty craters. May your bed above be aisy darlin', for the day's work ye are doon!—Whoosh! there ye are, and bedad, it's hard tellin' which is the dirtiest, the fut or the shoe." It was; and if he hadn't been to the fore, I should have gone on pulling, under the impression that the "fut" was a boot, for trousers, socks, shoes and legs were a mass of mud. This comical tableau produced a general grin, at which propitious beginning I took heart and scrubbed away like any tidy parent on a Saturday night. Some of them took the performance like sleepy children, leaning their tired heads against me as I worked, others looked grimly scandalized, and several of the roughest colored like bashful girls. One wore a soiled little bag about his neck, and, as I moved it, to bathe his wounded breast, I said,

"Your talisman didn't save you, did it?"

"Well, I reckon it did, marm, for that shot would a gone a couple a inches deeper but for my old mammy's camphor bag," answered the cheerful philosopher.

Another, with a gun-shot wound through the cheek, asked for a looking-glass, and when I brought one, regarded his swollen face with a dolorous expression, as he muttered—

"I vow to gosh, that's too bad! I warn't a bad looking chap before, and now I'm done for; won't there be a thunderin' scar? and what on earth will Josephine Skinner say?"

He looked up at me with his one eye so appealingly, that I controlled my risibles,[20] and assured him that if Josephine was a girl of

---

[19]vi et armis: Latin for "by force and arms" or "by main force."
[20]*risibles:* Tendency to laugh.

sense, she would admire the honorable scar, as a lasting proof that he had faced the enemy, for all women thought a wound the best decoration a brave soldier could wear. I hope Miss Skinner verified the good opinion I so rashly expressed of her, but I shall never know.

The next scrubbee was a nice looking lad, with a curly brown mane, and a budding trace of gingerbread over the lip, which he called his beard, and defended stoutly, when the barber jocosely suggested its immolation. He lay on a bed, with one leg gone, and the right arm so shattered that it must evidently follow; yet the little Sergeant was as merry as if his afflictions were not worth lamenting over, and when a drop or two of salt water mingled with my suds at the sight of this strong young body, so marred and maimed, the boy looked up, with a brave smile, though there was a little quiver of the lips, as he said,

"Now don't you fret yourself about me, miss; I'm first rate here, for it's nuts to lie still on this bed, after knocking about in those confounded ambulances, that shake what there is left of a fellow to jelly. I never was in one of these places before, and think this cleaning up a jolly thing for us, though I'm afraid it isn't for you ladies."

"Is this your first battle, Sergeant?"

"No, miss; I've been in six scrimmages, and never got a scratch till this last one; but it's done the business pretty thoroughly for me, I should say. Lord! what a scramble there'll be for arms and legs, when we old boys come out of our graves, on the Judgment Day: wonder if we shall get our own again? If we do, my leg will have to tramp from Fredericksburg, my arm from here, I suppose, and meet my body, wherever it may be."

The fancy seemed to tickle him mightily, for he laughed blithely, and so did I; which, no doubt, caused the new nurse to be regarded as a light-minded sinner by the Chaplain, who roamed vaguely about, informing the men that they were all worms, corrupt of heart, with perishable bodies, and souls only to be saved by a diligent perusal of certain tracts, and other equally cheering bits of spiritual consolation, when spirituous ditto[21] would have been preferred.

"I say, Mrs.!" called a voice behind me; and, turning, I saw a rough Michigander, with an arm blown off at the shoulder, and two or three bullets still in him—as he afterwards mentioned, as carelessly as if gentlemen were in the habit of carrying such trifles about with them. I went to him, and, while administering a dose of soap and water, he whispered, irefully:

---

[21]*spirituous ditto:* Alcoholic consolation.

"That red-headed devil, over yonder, is a reb, damn him! You'll agree to that, I'll bet? He's got shet of a foot, or he'd a cut like the rest of the lot. Don't you wash him, nor feed him, but jest let him holler till he's tired. It's a blasted shame to fetch them fellers in here, along side of us; and so I'll tell the chap that bosses this concern; cuss me if I don't."

I regret to say that I did not deliver a moral sermon upon the duty of forgiving our enemies, and the sin of profanity, then and there; but, being a red-hot Abolitionist, stared fixedly at the tall rebel, who was a copperhead,[22] in every sense of the word, and privately resolved to put soap in his eyes, rub his nose the wrong way, and excoriate his cuticle generally, if I had the washing of him.

My amiable intentions, however, were frustrated; for, when I approached, with as Christian an expression as my principles would allow, and asked the question — "Shall I try to make you more comfortable, sir?" all I got for my pains was a gruff—

"No; I'll do it myself."

"Here's your Southern chivalry, with a witness," thought I, dumping the basin down before him, thereby quenching a strong desire to give him a summary baptism, in return for his ungraciousness; for my angry passions rose, at this rebuff, in a way that would have scandalized good Dr. Watts. He was a disappointment in all respects, (the rebel, not the blessed Doctor,) for he was neither fiendish, romantic, pathetic, or anything interesting; but a long, fat man, with a head like a burning bush, and a perfectly expressionless face: so I could hate him without the slightest drawback, and ignored his existence from that day forth. One redeeming trait he certainly did possess, as the floor speedily testified; for his ablutions were so vigorously performed, that his bed soon stood like an isolated island, in a sea of soap-suds, and he resembled a dripping merman, suffering from the loss of a fin. If cleanliness is a near neighbor to godliness, then was the big rebel the godliest man in my ward that day.

Having done up our human wash, and laid it out to dry, the second syllable of our version of the word war-fare was enacted with much success. Great trays of bread, meat, soup and coffee appeared; and both nurses and attendants turned waiters, serving bountiful rations to all who could eat. I can call my pinafore to testify to my good will in

---

[22] *copperhead:* Word play referring both to the rebel's red hair and to the term *Copperhead,* which during the war often referred to antiwar Democrats. Copperheads opposed the emancipation of slaves and the employment of African Americans as soldiers.

the work, for in ten minutes it was reduced to a perambulating bill of fare, presenting samples of all the refreshments going or gone. It was a lively scene; the long room lined with rows of beds, each filled by an occupant, whom water, shears, and clean raiment, had transformed from a dismal ragamuffin into a recumbent hero, with a cropped head. To and fro rushed matrons, maids, and convalescent "boys,"[23] skirmishing with knives and forks; retreating with empty plates; marching and counter-marching, with unvaried success, while the clash of busy spoons made most inspiring music for the charge of our Light Brigade:[24]

> "Beds to the front of them,
> Beds to the right of them,
> Beds to the left of them,
>     Nobody blundered.
> Beamed at by hungry souls,
> Screamed at with brimming bowls,
> Steamed at by army rolls,
>     Buttered and sundered.
> With coffee not cannon plied,
> Each must be satisfied,
> Whether they lived or died;
>     All the men wondered."

Very welcome seemed the generous meal, after a week of suffering, exposure, and short commons;[25] soon the brown faces began to smile, as food, warmth, and rest, did their pleasant work; and the grateful "Thankee's" were followed by more graphic accounts of the battle and retreat, than any paid reporter could have given us. Curious contrasts of the tragic and comic met one everywhere; and some touching as well as ludicrous episodes, might have been recorded that

[23] *convalescent "boys":* It was standard practice during the war to employ convalescing soldiers as hospital attendants.

[24] Alcott parodies lines from Alfred, Lord Tennyson's famous poem on the Crimean War, "Charge of the Light Brigade," published in 1855. A verse from the original reads:
> Cannon to right of them,
> Cannon to left of them,
> Cannon in front of them
>     Volley'd and thunder'd;
> Stormed at with shot and shell,
> Boldly they rode and well,
> Into the jaws of Death,
> Into the mouth of Hell,
>     Rode the six hundred.

[25] *short commons:* Food or rations.

day. A six foot New Hampshire man, with a leg broken and perforated by a piece of shell, so large that, had I not seen the wound, I should have regarded the story as a Munchausenism, beckoned me to come and help him, as he could not sit up, and both his bed and beard were getting plentifully anointed with soup. As I fed my big nestling with corresponding mouthfuls, I asked him how he felt during the battle.

"Well, 'twas my fust, you see, so I aint ashamed to say I was a trifle flustered in the beginnin', there was such an allfired racket; for ef there's anything I do spleen agin,[26] it's noise. But when my mate, Eph Sylvester, caved, with a bullet through his head, I got mad, and pitched in, licketty cut. Our part of the fight didn't last long; so a lot of us larked round Fredericksburg, and give some of them houses a pretty consid'able of a rummage,[27] till we was ordered out of the mess. Some of our fellows cut like time; but I warn't a-goin to run for nobody; and, fust thing I knew, a shell bust, right in front of us, and I keeled over, feelin' as if I was blowed higher'n a kite. I sung out, and the boys come back for me, double quick; but the way they chucked me over them fences was a caution, I tell you. Next day I was most as black as that darkey yonder, lickin' plates on the sly. This is bully coffee, ain't it? Give us another pull at it, and I'll be obleeged to you."

I did; and, as the last gulp subsided, he said, with a rub of his old handkerchief over eyes as well as mouth:

"Look a here; I've got a pair a earbobs and a handkercher pin I'm a goin' to give you, if you'll have them; for you're the very moral o' Lizy Sylvester, poor Eph's wife: that's why I signalled you to come over here. They aint much, I guess, but they'll do to memorize the rebs by."

Burrowing under his pillow, he produced a little bundle of what he called "truck," and gallantly presented me with a pair of earrings, each representing a cluster of corpulent grapes, and the pin a basket of astonishing fruit, the whole large and coppery enough for a small warming-pan. Feeling delicate about depriving him of such valuable relics, I accepted the earrings alone, and was obliged to depart, somewhat abruptly, when my friend stuck the warming-pan in the bosom of his night-gown, viewing it with much complacency, and, perhaps some tender memory, in that rough heart of his, for the comrade he had lost.

---

[26]*spleen agin:* Dislike; complain about.

[27]Just before the Battle of Fredericksburg, Northern soldiers looted the evacuated town, destroying or removing furniture, glassware, and the like. Looting and "foraging" by both armies was common during the Civil War.

Observing that the man next him had left his meal untouched, I offered the same service I had performed for his neighbor, but he shook his head.

"Thank you, ma'am; I don't think I'll ever eat again, for I'm shot in the stomach. But I'd like a drink of water, if you aint too busy."

I rushed away, but the water-pails were gone to be refilled, and it was some time before they reappeared. I did not forget my patient patient, meanwhile, and, with the first mugful, hurried back to him. He seemed asleep; but something in the tired white face caused me to listen at his lips for a breath. None came. I touched his forehead; it was cold: and then I knew that, while he waited, a better nurse than I had given him a cooler draught, and healed him with a touch. I laid the sheet over the quiet sleeper, whom no noise could now disturb; and, half an hour later, the bed was empty. It seemed a poor requital for all he had sacrificed and suffered, — that hospital bed, lonely even in a crowd; for there was no familiar face for him to look his last upon; no friendly voice to say, Good bye; no hand to lead him gently down into the Valley of the Shadow; and he vanished, like a drop in that red sea upon whose shores so many women stand lamenting. For a moment I felt bitterly indignant at this seeming carelessness of the value of life, the sanctity of death; then consoled myself with the thought that, when the great muster roll was called, these nameless men might be promoted above many whose tall monuments record the barren honors they have won.

All having eaten, drank, and rested, the surgeons began their rounds; and I took my first lesson in the art of dressing wounds. It wasn't a festive scene, by any means; for Dr. P., whose Aid I constituted myself, fell to work with a vigor which soon convinced me that I was a weaker vessel, though nothing would have induced me to confess it then. He had served in the Crimea, and seemed to regard a dilapidated body very much as I should have regarded a damaged garment; and, turning up his cuffs, whipped out a very unpleasant looking housewife,[28] cutting, sawing, patching and piecing, with the enthusiasm of an accomplished surgical seamstress; explaining the process, in scientific terms, to the patient, meantime; which, of course, was immensely cheering and comfortable. There was an uncanny sort of fascination in watching him, as he peered and probed into the mechanism of those wonderful bodies, whose mysteries he understood so well. The more intricate the wound, the better he liked it. A

---

[28] *housewife:* Sewing kit issued to soldiers.

poor private, with both legs cut off, and shot through the lungs, possessed more attractions for him than a dozen generals, slightly
scratched in some "masterly retreat;" and had any one appeared in
small pieces, requesting to be put together again, he would have considered it a special dispensation.

The amputations were reserved till the morrow, and the merciful
magic of ether was not thought necessary that day, so the poor souls
had to bear their pains as best they might. It is all very well to talk of
the patience of woman; and far be it from me to pluck that feather
from her cap, for, heaven knows, she isn't allowed to wear many; but
the patient endurance of these men, under trials of the flesh, was truly
wonderful; their fortitude seemed contagious, and scarcely a cry
escaped them, though I often longed to groan for them, when pride
kept their white lips shut, while great drops stood upon their fore-
heads, and the bed shook with the irrepressible tremor of their tor-
tured bodies. One or two Irishmen anathematized the doctors with the
frankness of their nation, and ordered the Virgin to stand by them, as
if she had been the wedded Biddy to whom they could administer the
poker, if she didn't;[29] but, as a general thing, the work went on in
silence, broken only by some quiet request for roller, instruments,
or plaster, a sigh from the patient, or a sympathizing murmur from
the nurse.

It was long past noon before these repairs were even partially
made; and, having got the bodies of my boys into something like
order, the next task was to minister to their minds, by writing letters
to the anxious souls at home; answering questions, reading papers,
taking possession of money and valuables; for the eighth command-
ment was reduced to a very fragmentary condition, both by the blacks
and whites, who ornamented our hospital with their presence. Pocket
books, purses, miniatures, and watches, were sealed up, labelled, and
handed over to the matron, till such times as the owners thereof were
ready to depart homeward or campward again. The letters dictated to
me, and revised by me, that afternoon, would have made an excellent
chapter for some future history of the war; for, like that which Thack-

[29]This passage reveals some of Alcott's ethnic stereotyping. *Biddy* was a colloquial
form of Bridget, used widely to name and often stigmatize Irish women servants in the
mid-nineteenth century. Similarly, Irish men were often called "Patrick" in a derogatory
way, no matter what their names. Here, Alcott assumes violence in Irish marriages, as
she imagines an Irish soldier's wife as "the wedded Biddy to whom they could administer the poker." Her reference to the Virgin is a shorthand means of referring to Catholicism, the religion of most Irish immigrants.

eray's "Ensign Spooney"[30] wrote his mother just before Waterloo, they were "full of affection, pluck, and bad spelling;" nearly all giving lively accounts of the battle, and ending with a somewhat sudden plunge from patriotism to provender, desiring "Marm," "Mary Ann," or "Aunt Peters," to send along some pies, pickles, sweet stuff, and apples, "to yourn in haste," Joe, Sam, or Ned, as the case might be.

My little Sergeant insisted on trying to scribble something with his left hand, and patiently accomplished some half dozen lines of hieroglyphics, which he gave me to fold and direct, with a boyish blush, that rendered a glimpse of "My Dearest Jane," unnecessary, to assure me that the heroic lad had been more successful in the service of Commander-in-Chief Cupid than that of Gen. Mars;[31] and a charming little romance blossomed instanter in Nurse Periwinkle's romantic fancy, though no further confidences were made that day, for Sergeant fell asleep, and, judging from his tranquil face, visited his absent sweetheart in the pleasant land of dreams.

At five o'clock a great bell rang, and the attendants flew, not to arms, but to their trays, to bring up supper, when a second uproar announced that it was ready. The new comers woke at the sound; and I presently discovered that it took a very bad wound to incapacitate the defenders of the faith for the consumption of their rations; the amount that some of them sequestered was amazing; but when I suggested the probability of a famine hereafter, to the matron, that motherly lady cried out: "Bless their hearts, why shouldn't they eat? It's their only amusement; so fill every one, and, if there's not enough ready to-night, I'll lend my share to the Lord by giving it to the boys." And, whipping up her coffee-pot and plate of toast, she gladdened the eyes and stomachs of two or three dissatisfied heroes; by serving them with a liberal hand; and I haven't the slightest doubt that, having cast her bread upon the waters, it came back buttered, as another large-hearted old lady was wont to say.

Then came the doctor's evening visit; the administration of medicines; washing feverish faces; smoothing tumbled beds; wetting wounds; singing lullabies; and preparations for the night. By eleven, the last labor of love was done; the last "good night" spoken; and, if

---

[30]*Ensign Spooney:* A callow young soldier in William Makepeace Thackeray's satirical 1848 novel, *Vanity Fair.* Alcott misquotes slightly: Spooney and a friend write "letters to the kind anxious parents at home—letters full of love and heartiness, and pluck and bad spelling."

[31]Mars was the Roman god of war, and Cupid the Roman god of love. Alcott here indicates that her "little Sergeant" has been more successful in love than war.

any needed a reward for that day's work, they surely received it, in the silent eloquence of those long lines of faces, showing pale and peaceful in the shaded rooms, as we quitted them, followed by grateful glances that lighted us to bed, where rest, the sweetest, made our pillows soft, while Night and Nature took our places, filling that great house of pain with the healing miracles of Sleep, and his diviner brother, Death.

## CHAPTER IV. A NIGHT

Being fond of the night side of nature, I was soon promoted to the post of night nurse, with every facility for indulging in my favorite pastime of "owling." My colleague, a black-eyed widow, relieved me at dawn, we two taking care of the ward, between us, like the immortal Sairy and Betsey,[32] "turn and turn about." I usually found my boys in the jolliest state of mind their condition allowed; for it was a known fact that Nurse Periwinkle objected to blue devils, and entertained a belief that he who laughed most was surest of recovery. At the beginning of my reign, dumps and dismals prevailed; the nurses looked anxious and tired, the men gloomy or sad; and a general "Hark! from-the-tombs-a-doleful-sound" style of conversation seemed to be the fashion: a state of things which caused one coming from a merry, social New England town, to feel as if she had got into an exhausted receiver; and the instinct of self-preservation, to say nothing of a philanthropic desire to serve the race, caused a speedy change in Ward No. 1.

More flattering than the most gracefully turned compliment, more grateful than the most admiring glance, was the sight of those rows of faces, all strange to me a little while ago, now lighting up, with smiles of welcome, as I came among them, enjoying that moment heartily, with a womanly pride in their regard, a motherly affection for them all. The evenings were spent in reading aloud, writing letters, waiting on and amusing the men, going the rounds with Dr. P., as he made his second daily survey, dressing my dozen wounds afresh, giving last doses, and making them cozy for the long hours to come, till the nine o'clock bell rang, the gas was turned down, the day nurses went off duty, the night watch came on, and my nocturnal adventure began.

My ward was now divided into three rooms; and, under favor of the

---

[32] *Sairy and Betsey:* Sairey Gamp is a character in Charles Dickens's *Martin Chuzzlewit.* Betsey Trotwood is David Copperfield's aunt in Dickens's *David Copperfield.*

matron, I had managed to sort out the patients in such a way that I had what I called, "my duty room," my "pleasure room," and my "pathetic room," and worked for each in a different way. One, I visited, armed with a dressing tray, full of rollers,[33] plasters, and pins; another, with books, flowers, games, and gossip; a third, with teapots, lullabies, consolation, and, sometimes, a shroud.

Wherever the sickest or most helpless man chanced to be, there I held my watch, often visiting the other rooms, to see that the general watchman of the ward did his duty by the fires and the wounds, the latter needing constant wetting. Not only on this account did I meander, but also to get fresher air than the close rooms afforded; for, owing to the stupidity of that mysterious "somebody" who does all the damage in the world, the windows had been carefully nailed down above, and the lower sashes could only be raised in the mildest weather, for the men lay just below. I had suggested a summary smashing of a few panes here and there, when frequent appeals to headquarters had proved unavailing, and daily orders to lazy attendants had come to nothing. No one seconded the motion, however, and the nails were far beyond my reach; for, though belonging to the sisterhood of "ministering angels," I had no wings, and might as well have asked for Jacob's ladder,[34] as a pair of steps, in that charitable chaos.

One of the harmless ghosts who bore me company during the haunted hours, was Dan, the watchman, whom I regarded with a certain awe; for, though so much together, I never fairly saw his face, and, but for his legs, should never have recognized him, as we seldom met by day. These legs were remarkable, as was his whole figure, for his body was short, rotund, and done up in a big jacket, and muffler; his beard hid the lower part of his face, his hat brim the upper; and all I ever discovered was a pair of sleepy eyes, and a very mild voice. But the legs!—very long, very thin, very crooked and feeble, looking like grey sausages in their tight coverings, without a ray of pegtopishness about them, and finished off with a pair of expansive, green cloth shoes, very like Chinese junks, with the sails down. This figure, gliding noiselessly about the dimly lighted rooms, was strongly suggestive of the spirit of a beer barrel mounted on cork-screws, haunting the old hotel in search of its lost mates, emptied and staved in long ago.

Another goblin who frequently appeared to me, was the attendant

---

[33] *rollers:* Bandage rollers.

[34] *Jacob's ladder:* A reference to the biblical story from the Book of Genesis in which Jacob dreamed that he saw a ladder reaching to heaven with angels ascending and descending.

of the pathetic room, who, being a faithful soul, was often up to tend two or three men, weak and wandering as babies, after the fever had gone. The amiable creature beguiled the watches of the night by brewing jorums of a fearful beverage, which he called coffee, and insisted on sharing with me; coming in with a great bowl of something like mud soup, scalding hot, guiltless of cream, rich in an all-pervading flavor of molasses, scorch and tin pot. Such an amount of good will and neighborly kindness also went into the mess, that I never could find the heart to refuse, but always received it with thanks, sipped it with hypocritical relish while he remained, and whipped it into the slop-jar the instant he departed, thereby gratifying him, securing one rousing laugh in the doziest hour of the night, and no one was the worse for the transaction but the pigs. Whether they were "cut off untimely in their sins," or not, I carefully abstained from inquiring.

It was a strange life—asleep half the day, exploring Washington the other half, and all night hovering, like a massive cherubim, in a red rigolette, over the slumbering sons of man. I liked it, and found many things to amuse, instruct, and interest me. The snores alone were quite a study, varying from the mild sniff to the stentorian snort, which startled the echoes and hoisted the performer erect to accuse his neighbor of the deed, magnanimously forgive him, and, wrapping the drapery of his couch about him, lie down to vocal slumber. After listening for a week to this band of wind instruments, I indulged in the belief that I could recognize each by the snore alone, and was tempted to join the chorus by breaking out with John Brown's favorite hymn:[35]

"Blow ye the trumpet, blow!"

I would have given much to have possessed the art of sketching, for many of the faces became wonderfully interesting when unconscious. Some grew stern and grim, the men evidently dreaming of war, as they gave orders, groaned over their wounds, or damned the rebels vigorously; some grew sad and infinitely pathetic, as if the pain borne silently all day, revenged itself by now betraying what the man's pride had concealed so well. Often the roughest grew young and

[35] John Brown was a militant abolitionist who, in 1859, led a small group of men in a raid on the federal arsenal at Harpers Ferry, with the hope that his attack would inspire a general uprising among slaves against slavery. Subsequently hanged for treason, Brown was widely seen as a martyr among antislavery activists in the North, while Southerners viewed Brown's actions as an indication that the North would not shy away from attacking the South to destroy the institution of slavery. The hymn is by Charles Wesley.

pleasant when sleep smoothed the hard lines away, letting the real nature assert itself; many almost seemed to speak, and I learned to know these men better by night than through any intercourse by day. Sometimes they disappointed me, for faces that looked merry and good in the light, grew bad and sly when the shadows came; and though they made no confidences in words, I read their lives, leaving them to wonder at the change of manner this midnight magic wrought in their nurse. A few talked busily; one drummer boy sang sweetly, though no persuasions could win a note from him by day; and several depended on being told what they had talked of in the morning. Even my constitutionals in the chilly halls, possessed a certain charm, for the house was never still. Sentinels tramped round it all night long, their muskets glittering in the wintry moonlight as they walked, or stood before the doors, straight and silent, as figures of stone, causing one to conjure up romantic visions of guarded forts, sudden surprises, and daring deeds; for in these war times the hum drum life of Yankee-dom has vanished, and the most prosaic feel some thrill of that excitement which stirs the nation's heart, and makes its capital a camp of hospitals. Wandering up and down these lower halls, I often heard cries from above, steps hurrying to and fro, saw surgeons passing up, or men coming down carrying a stretcher, where lay a long white figure, whose face was shrouded and whose fight was done. Sometimes I stopped to watch the passers in the street, the moonlight shining on the spire opposite, or the gleam of some vessel floating, like a white-winged sea-gull, down the broad Potomac, whose fullest flow can never wash away the red stain of the land.

The night whose events I have a fancy to record, opened with a little comedy, and closed with a great tragedy; for a virtuous and useful life untimely ended is always tragical to those who see not as God sees. My headquarters were beside the bed of a New Jersey boy, crazed by the horrors of that dreadful Saturday. A slight wound in the knee brought him there; but his mind had suffered more than his body; some string of that delicate machine was over strained, and, for days, he had been reliving, in imagination, the scenes he could not forget, till his distress broke out in incoherent ravings, pitiful to hear. As I sat by him, endeavoring to soothe his poor distracted brain by the constant touch of wet hands over his hot forehead, he lay cheering his comrades on, hurrying them back, then counting them as they fell around him, often clutching my arm, to drag me from the vicinity of a bursting shell, or covering up his head to screen himself from a shower of shot; his face brilliant with fever; his eyes restless; his head never still; every muscle strained and rigid; while an incessant stream of defiant shouts, whispered warnings, and broken laments, poured from his lips with that forceful bewilderment which makes such wanderings so hard to overhear.

It was past eleven, and my patient was slowly wearying himself into fitful intervals of quietude, when, in one of these pauses, a curious sound arrested my attention. Looking over my shoulder, I saw a one-legged phantom hopping nimbly down the room; and, going to meet it, recognized a certain Pennsylvania gentleman, whose wound-fever had taken a turn for the worse, and, depriving him of the few wits a drunken campaign had left him, set him literally tripping on the light, fantastic toe "toward home," as he blandly informed me, touching the military cap which formed a striking contrast to the severe simplicity of the rest of his decidedly *undress* uniform. When sane, the least movement produced a roar of pain or a volley of oaths; but the departure of reason seemed to have wrought an agreeable change, both in the man and his manners; for, balancing himself on one leg, like a meditative stork, he plunged into an animated discussion of the war, the President, lager beer, and Enfield rifles, regardless of any suggestions of mine as to the propriety of returning to bed, lest he be court-martialed for desertion.

Anything more supremely ridiculous can hardly be imagined than this figure, scantily draped in white, its one foot covered with a big blue sock, a dingy cap set rakingly askew on its shaven head, and placid satisfaction beaming in its broad red face, as it flourished a mug in one hand, an old boot in the other, calling them canteen and knapsack, while it skipped and fluttered in the most unearthly fashion. What to do with the creature I didn't know; Dan was absent, and if I went to find him, the perambulator might festoon himself out of the window, set his toga on fire, or do some of his neighbors a mischief. The attendant of the room was sleeping like a near relative of the celebrated Seven, and nothing short of pins would rouse him; for he had been out that day, and whiskey asserted its supremacy in balmy whiffs. Still declaiming, in a fine flow of eloquence, the demented gentleman hopped on, blind and deaf to my graspings and entreaties; and I was about to slam the door in his face, and run for help, when a second and saner phantom, "all in white," came to the rescue, in the likeness of a big Prussian, who spoke no English, but divined the crisis, and put an end to it, by bundling the lively monoped into his bed, like a baby, with an authoritative command to "stay put," which received added weight from being delivered in an odd conglomeration of

French and German, accompanied by warning wags of a head decorated with a yellow cotton night cap, rendered most imposing by a tassel like a bell-pull. Rather exhausted by his excursion, the member from Pennsylvania subsided; and, after an irrepressible laugh together, my Prussian ally and myself were returning to our places, when the echo of a sob caused us to glance along the beds. It came from one in the corner—such a little bed!—and such a tearful little face looked up at us, as we stopped beside it! The twelve years old drummer boy was not singing now, but sobbing, with a manly effort all the while to stifle the distressful sounds that would break out.

"What is it, Teddy?" I asked, as he rubbed the tears away, and checked himself in the middle of a great sob to answer plaintively:

"I've got a chill, ma'am, but I aint cryin' for that, 'cause I'm used to it. I dreamed Kit was here, and when I waked up he wasn't, and I couldn't help it, then."

The boy came in with the rest, and the man who was taken dead from the ambulance was the Kit he mourned. Well he might; for, when the wounded were brought from Fredericksburg, the child lay in one of the camps thereabout, and this good friend, though sorely hurt himself, would not leave him to the exposure and neglect of such a time and place; but, wrapping him in his own blanket, carried him in his arms to the transport, tended him during the passage, and only yielded up his charge when Death met him at the door of the hospital which promised care and comfort for the boy. For ten days, Teddy had shivered or burned with fever and ague, pining the while for Kit, and refusing to be comforted, because he had not been able to thank him for the generous protection, which, perhaps, had cost the giver's life. The vivid dream had wrung the childish heart with a fresh pang, and when I tried the solace fitted for his years, the remorseful fear that haunted him found vent in a fresh burst of tears, as he looked at the wasted hands I was endeavoring to warm:

"Oh! if I'd only been as thin when Kit carried me as I am now, maybe he wouldn't have died; but I was heavy, he was hurt worser than we knew, and so it killed him; and I didn't see him, to say good bye."

This thought had troubled him in secret; and my assurances that his friend would probably have died at all events, hardly assuaged the bitterness of his regretful grief.

At this juncture, the delirious man began to shout; the one-legged rose up in his bed, as if preparing for another dart; Teddy bewailed himself more piteously than before: and if ever a woman was at her wit's end, that distracted female was Nurse Periwinkle, during the space of two or three minutes, as she vibrated between the three beds, like an agitated pendulum. Like a most opportune reinforcement, Dan, the bandy, appeared, and devoted himself to the lively party, leaving me free to return to my post; for the Prussian, with a nod and a smile, took the lad away to his own bed, and lulled him to sleep with a soothing murmur, like a mammoth bumble bee. I liked that in Fritz, and if he ever wondered afterward at the dainties which sometimes found their way into his rations, or the extra comforts of his bed, he might have found a solution of the mystery in sundry persons' knowledge of the fatherly action of that night.

Hardly was I settled again, when the inevitable bowl appeared, and its bearer delivered a message I had expected, yet dreaded to receive:

"John is going, ma'am, and wants to see you, if you can come."

"The moment this boy is asleep; tell him so, and let me know if I am in danger of being too late."

My Ganymede[36] departed, and while I quieted poor Shaw, I thought of John. He came in a day or two after the others; and, one evening, when I entered my "pathetic room," I found a lately emptied bed occupied by a large, fair man, with a fine face, and the serenest eyes I ever met. One of the earlier comers had often spoken of a friend, who had remained behind, that those apparently worse wounded than himself might reach a shelter first. It seemed a David and Jonathan sort of friendship.[37] The man fretted for his mate, and was never tired of praising John—his courage, sobriety, self-denial, and unfailing kindliness of heart; always winding up with: "He's an out an' out fine feller, ma'am; you see if he aint."

I had some curiosity to behold this piece of excellence, and when he came, watched him for a night or two, before I made friends with him; for, to tell the truth, I was a little afraid of the stately looking man, whose bed had to be lengthened to accommodate his commanding stature; who seldom spoke, uttered no complaint, asked no sympathy, but tranquilly observed what went on about him; and, as he lay high upon his pillows, no picture of dying statesman or warrior was ever fuller of real dignity than this Virginia blacksmith. A most attractive face he had, framed in brown hair and beard, comely featured and full of vigor, as yet unsubdued by pain; thoughtful and often beautifully mild while watching the afflictions of others, as if entirely forgetful of his own. His mouth was grave and firm, with plenty of will and

---

[36] *Ganymede:* In Greek mythology, cupbearer of the gods.
[37] A famous biblical friendship.

courage in its lines, but a smile could make it as sweet as any woman's; and his eyes were child's eyes, looking one fairly in the face, with a clear, straightforward glance, which promised well for such as placed their faith in him. He seemed to cling to life, as if it were rich in duties and delights, and he had learned the secret of content. The only time I saw his composure disturbed, was when my surgeon brought another to examine John, who scrutinized their faces with an anxious look, asking of the elder: "Do you think I shall pull through, sir?" "I hope so, my man." And, as the two passed on John's eye still followed them, with an intentness which would have won a clearer answer from them, had they seen it. A momentary shadow flitted over his face; then came the usual serenity, as if, in that brief eclipse, he had acknowledged the existence of some hard possibility, and, asking nothing yet hoping all things, left the issue in God's hands, with that submission which is true piety.

The next night, as I went my rounds with Dr. P., I happened to ask which man in the room probably suffered most; and, to my great surprise, he glanced at John:

"Every breath he draws is like a stab; for the ball pierced the left lung, broke a rib, and did no end of damage here and there; so the poor lad can find neither forgetfulness nor ease, because he must lie on his wounded back or suffocate. It will be a hard struggle, and a long one, for he possesses great vitality; but even his temperate life can't save him; I wish it could."

"You don't mean he must die, Doctor?"

"Bless you, there's not the slightest hope for him; and you'd better tell him so before long; women have a way of doing such things comfortably, so I leave it to you. He won't last more than a day or two, at furthest."

I could have sat down on the spot and cried heartily; if I had not learned the wisdom of bottling up one's tears for leisure moments. Such an end seemed very hard for such a man, when half a dozen worn out, worthless bodies round him, were gathering up the remnants of wasted lives, to linger on for years perhaps, burdens to others, daily reproaches to themselves. The army needed men like John, earnest, brave, and faithful; fighting for liberty and justice with both heart and hand, true soldiers of the Lord. I could not give him up so soon, or think with any patience of so excellent a nature robbed of its fulfillment, and blundered into eternity by the rashness or stupidity of those at whose hands so many lives may be required. It was an easy thing for Dr. P. to say: "Tell him he must die," but a cruelly hard thing to do, and by no means as "comfortable" as he politely suggested. I had not the heart to do it then, and privately indulged the hope that some change for the better might take place, in spite of gloomy prophesies; so, rendering my task unnecessary. A few minutes later, as I came in again, with fresh rollers, I saw John sitting erect, with no one to support him, while the surgeon dressed his back. I had never hitherto seen it done; for, having simpler wounds to attend to, and knowing the fidelity of the attendant, I had left John to him, thinking it might be more agreeable and safe; for both strength and experience were needed in his case. I had forgotten that the strong man might long for the gentler tendance of a woman's hands, the sympathetic magnetism of a woman's presence, as well as the feebler souls about him. The Doctor's words caused me to reproach myself with neglect, not of any real duty perhaps, but of those little cares and kindnesses that solace homesick spirits, and make the heavy hours pass easier. John looked lonely and forsaken just then, as he sat with bent head, hands folded on his knee, and no outward sign of suffering, till, looking nearer, I saw great tears roll down and drop upon the floor. It was a new sight there; for, though I had seen many suffer, some swore, some groaned, most endured silently, but none wept. Yet it did not seem weak, only very touching, and straightway my fear vanished, my heart opened wide and took him in, as, gathering the bent head in my arms, as freely as if he had been a little child, I said, "Let me help you bear it, John."

Never, on any human countenance, have I seen so swift and beautiful a look of gratitude, surprise and comfort, as that which answered me more eloquently than the whispered—

"Thank you, ma'am, this is right good! this is what I wanted!"

"Then why not ask for it before?"

"I didn't like to be a trouble; you seemed so busy, and I could manage to get on alone."

"You shall not want it any more, John."

Nor did he; for now I understood the wistful look that sometimes followed me, as I went out, after a brief pause beside his bed, or merely a passing nod, while busied with those who seemed to need me more than he, because more urgent in their demands; now I knew that to him, as to so many, I was the poor substitute for mother, wife, or sister, and in his eyes no stranger, but a friend who hitherto had seemed neglectful; for, in his modesty, he had never guessed the truth. This was changed now; and, through the tedious operation of probing, bathing, and dressing his wounds, he leaned against me, holding my hand fast, and, if pain wrung further tears from him, no one saw them fall but me. When he was laid down again, I hovered about him, in a remorseful state of mind that would not let me rest, till I had bathed his face, brushed his "bonny brown hair," set all things smooth about him, and laid a knot of heath and heliotrope on his clean pillow. While doing this, he watched me with the satisfied expression I so liked to see; and when I offered the little nosegay, held it carefully in his great hand, smoothed a ruffled leaf or two, surveyed and smelt it with an air of genuine delight, and lay contentedly regarding the glimmer of the sunshine on the green. Although the manliest man among my forty, he said, "Yes, ma'am," like a little boy; received suggestions for his comfort with the quick smile that brightened his whole face; and now and then, as I stood tidying the table by his bed, I felt him softly touch my gown, as if to assure himself that I was there. Anything more natural and frank I never saw, and found this brave John as bashful as brave, yet full of excellencies and fine aspirations, which, having no power to express themselves in words, seemed to have bloomed into his character and made him what he was.

After that night, an hour of each evening that remained to him was devoted to his ease or pleasure. He could not talk much, for breath was precious, and he spoke in whispers; but from occasional conversations, I gleaned scraps of private history which only added to the affection and respect I felt for him. Once he asked me to write a letter, and as I settled pen and paper, I said, with an irrepressible glimmer of feminine curiosity, "Shall it be addressed to wife, or mother, John?"

"Neither, ma'am; I've got no wife, and will write to mother myself when I get better. Did you think I was married because of this?" he asked, touching a plain ring he wore, and often turned thoughtfully on his finger when he lay alone.

"Partly that, but more from a settled sort of look you have, a look which young men seldom get until they marry."

"I don't know that; but I'm not so very young, ma'am, thirty in May, and have been what you might call settled this ten years; for mother's a widow, I'm the oldest child she has, and it wouldn't do for me to marry until Lizzy has a home of her own, and Laurie's learned his trade; for we're not rich, and I must be father to the children and husband to the dear old woman, if I can."

"No doubt but you are both, John; yet how came you to go to war, if you felt so? Wasn't enlisting as bad as marrying?"

"No, ma'am, not as I see it, for one is helping my neighbor, the other pleasing myself. I went because I couldn't help it. I didn't want the glory or the pay; I wanted the right thing done, and people kept saying the men who were in earnest ought to fight. I was in earnest, the Lord knows! but I held off as long as I could, not knowing which was my duty; mother saw the case, gave me her ring to keep me steady, and said 'Go:' so I went."

A short story and a simple one, but the man and the mother were portrayed better than pages of fine writing could have done it.

"Do you ever regret that you came, when you lie here suffering so much?"

"Never, ma'am; I haven't helped a great deal, but I've shown I was willing to give my life, and perhaps I've got to; but I don't blame anybody, and if it was to do over again, I'd do it. I'm a little sorry I wasn't wounded in front; it looks cowardly to be hit in the back, but I obeyed orders, and it don't matter in the end, I know."

Poor John! it did not matter now, except that a shot in front might have spared the long agony in store for him. He seemed to read the thought that troubled me, as he spoke so hopefully when there was no hope, for he suddenly added:

"This is my first battle; do they think it's going to be my last?"

"I'm afraid they do, John."

It was the hardest question I had ever been called upon to answer; doubly hard with those clear eyes fixed on mine, forcing a truthful answer by their own truth. He seemed a little startled at first, pondered over the fateful fact a moment then shook his head, with a glance at the broad chest and muscular limbs stretched out before him:

"I'm not afraid, but it's difficult to believe all at once. I'm so strong it don't seem possible for such a little wound to kill me."

Merry Mercutio's dying words[38] glanced through my memory as he spoke: "'Tis not so deep as a well, nor so wide as a church door, but 'tis enough." And John would have said the same could he have seen the ominous black holes between his shoulders, he never had; and, seeing the ghastly sights about him, could not believe his own wound more fatal than these, for all the suffering it caused him.

"Shall I write to your mother, now?" I asked, thinking that these sudden tidings might change all plans and purposes; but they did not; for the man received the order of the Divine Commander to march with the same unquestioning obedience with which the soldier had

---

[38]Alcott quotes from Mercutio's famous speech in Shakespeare's *Romeo and Juliet*, after Mercutio has received a fatal wound.

received that of the human one, doubtless remembering that the first led him to life, and the last to death.

"No, ma'am; to Laurie just the same; he'll break it to her best, and I'll add a line to her myself when you get done."

So I wrote the letter which he dictated, finding it better than any I had sent; for, though here and there a little ungrammatical or inelegant, each sentence came to me briefly worded, but most expressive; full of excellent counsel to the boy, tenderly bequeathing "mother and Lizzie" to his care, and bidding him good bye in words the sadder for their simplicity. He added a few lines, with steady hand, and, as I sealed it, said, with a patient sort of sigh, "I hope the answer will come in time for me to see it;" then, turning away his face, laid the flowers against his lips, as if to hide some quiver of emotion at the thought of such a sudden sundering of all the dear home ties.

These things had happened two days before; now John was dying, and the letter had not come. I had been summoned to many death beds in my life, but to none that made my heart ache as it did then, since my mother called me to watch the departure of a spirit akin to this in its gentleness and patient strength. As I went in, John stretched out both hands:

"I knew you'd come! I guess I'm moving on, ma'am."

He was; and so rapidly that, even while he spoke, over his face I saw the grey veil falling that no human hand can lift. I sat down by him, wiped the drops from his forehead, stirred the air about him with the slow wave of a fan, and waited to help him die. He stood in sore need of help—and I could do so little; for, as the doctor had foretold, the strong body rebelled against death, and fought every inch of the way, forcing him to draw each breath with a spasm, and clench his hands with an imploring look, as if he asked, "How long must I endure this, and be still!" For hours he suffered dumbly, without a moment's respite, or a moment's murmuring; his limbs grew cold, his face damp, his lips white, and, again and again, he tore the covering off his breast, as if the lightest weight added to his agony; yet through it all, his eyes never lost their perfect serenity, and the man's soul seemed to sit therein, undaunted by the ills that vexed his flesh.

One by one, the men woke, and round the room appeared a circle of pale faces and watchful eyes, full of awe and pity; for, though a stranger, John was beloved by all. Each man there had wondered at his patience, respected his piety, admired his fortitude, and now lamented his hard death; for the influence of an upright nature had made itself deeply felt, even in one little week. Presently, the Jonathan who so loved this comely David, came creeping from his bed for a last look and word. The kind soul was full of trouble, as the choke in his voice, the grasp of his hand, betrayed; but there were no tears, and the farewell of the friends was the more touching for its brevity.

"Old boy, how are you?" faltered the one.

"Most through, thank heaven!" whispered the other.

"Can I say or do anything for you anywheres?"

"Take my things home, and tell them that I did my best."

"I will! I will!"

"Good bye, Ned."

"Good bye, John, good bye!"

They kissed each other, tenderly as women, and so parted, for poor Ned could not stay to see his comrade die. For a little while, there was no sound in the room but the drip of water, from a stump or two, and John's distressful gasps, as he slowly breathed his life away. I thought him nearly gone, and had just laid down the fan, believing its help to be no longer needed, when suddenly he rose up in his bed, and cried out with a bitter cry that broke the silence, sharply startling everyone with its agonized appeal:

"For God's sake, give me air!"

It was the only cry pain or death had wrung from him, the only boon he had asked; and none of us could grant it, for all the airs that blew were useless now. Dan flung up the window. The first red streak of dawn was warming the grey east, a herald of the coming sun; John saw it, and with the love of light which lingers in us to the end, seemed to read in it a sign of hope of help, for, over his whole face there broke that mysterious expression, brighter than any smile, which often comes to eyes that look their last. He laid himself gently down; and, stretching out his strong right arm, as if to grasp and bring the blessed air to his lips in a fuller flow, lapsed into a merciful unconsciousness, which assured us that for him suffering was forever past. He died then; for, though the heavy breaths still tore their way up for a little longer, they were but the waves of an ebbing tide that beat unfelt against the wreck, which an immortal voyager had deserted with a smile. He never spoke again, but to the end held my hand close, so close that when he was asleep at last, I could not draw it away. Dan helped me, warning me as he did so that it was unsafe for dead and living flesh to lie so long together; but though my hand was strangely cold and stiff, and four white marks remained across its back, even when warmth and color had returned elsewhere, I could not but be glad that, through its touch, the presence of human sympathy, perhaps, had lightened that hard hour.

When they had made him ready for the grave, John lay in state for half an hour, a thing which seldom happened in that busy place; but a universal sentiment of reverence and affection seemed to fill the hearts of all who had known or heard of him; and when the rumor of his death went through the house, always astir, many came to see him, and I felt a tender sort of pride in my lost patient; for he looked a most heroic figure, lying there stately and still as the statue of some young knight asleep upon his tomb. The lovely expression which so often beautifies dead faces, soon replaced the marks of pain, and I longed for those who loved him best to see him when half an hour's acquaintance with Death had made them friends. As we stood looking at him, the ward master handed me a letter, saying it had been forgotten the night before. It was John's letter, come just an hour too late to gladden the eyes that had longed and looked for it so eagerly: yet he had it; for, after I had cut some brown locks for his mother, and taken off the ring to send her, telling how well the talisman had done its work, I kissed this good son for her sake, and laid the letter in his hand, still folded as when I drew my own away, feeling that its place was there, and making myself happy with the thought, that, even in his solitary place in the "Government Lot," he would not be without some token of the love which makes life beautiful and outlives death. Then I left him, glad to have known so genuine a man, and carrying with me an enduring memory of the brave Virginia blacksmith, as he lay serenely waiting for the dawn of that long day which knows no night.

## CHAPTER V. OFF DUTY

"My dear girl, we shall have you sick in your bed, unless you keep yourself warm and quiet for a few days. Widow Wadman can take care of the ward alone, now the men are so comfortable, and have her vacation when you are about again. Now do be prudent in time, and don't let me have to add a Periwinkle to my bouquet of patients."

This advice was delivered, in a paternal manner, by the youngest surgeon in the hospital, a kind-hearted little gentleman, who seemed to consider me a frail young blossom, that needed much cherishing, instead of a tough old spinster, who had been knocking about the world for thirty years. At the time I write of, he discovered me sitting on the stairs, with a nice cloud of unwholesome steam rising from the washroom; a party of January breezes disporting themselves in the halls; and perfumes, by no means from "Araby the blest,"[39] keeping them company; while I enjoyed a fit of coughing, which caused my head to spin in a way that made the application of a cool banister both necessary and agreeable, as I waited for the frolicsome wind to restore the breath I'd lost; cheering myself, meantime, with a secret conviction that pneumonia was waiting for me round the corner. This piece of advice had been offered by several persons for a week, and refused by me with the obstinacy with which my sex is so richly gifted. But the last few hours had developed several surprising internal and external phenomena, which impressed upon me the fact that if I didn't make a masterly retreat very soon, I should tumble down somewhere, and have to be borne ignominiously from the field. My head felt like a cannon ball; my feet had a tendency to cleave to the floor; the walls at times undulated in a most disagreeable manner; people looked unnaturally big; and the "very bottles on the mankle [mantel] shelf" appeared to dance derisively before my eyes. Taking these things into consideration, while blinking stupidly at Dr. Z., I resolved to retire gracefully, if I must; so, with a valedictory to my boys, a private lecture to Mrs. Wadman, and a fervent wish that I could take off my body and work in my soul, I mournfully ascended to my apartment, and Nurse P. was reported off duty.

For the benefit of any ardent damsel whose patriotic fancy may have surrounded hospital life with a halo of charms, I will briefly describe the bower to which I retired, in a somewhat ruinous condition. It was well ventilated, for five panes of glass had suffered compound fractures, which all the surgeons and nurses had failed to heal; the two windows were draped with sheets, the church hospital opposite being a brick and mortar Argus,[40] and the female mind cherishing a prejudice in favor of retiracy during the night-capped periods of existence. A bare floor supported two narrow iron beds, spread with thin mattresses like plasters, furnished with pillows in the last stages of consumption. In a fire place, guiltless of shovel, tongs, andirons, or grate, burned a log, inch by inch, being too long to go on all at once; so, while the fire blazed away at one end, I did the same at the other, as I tripped over it a dozen times a day, and flew up to poke it a dozen

---

[39]"Araby the blest": A quotation from John Milton's *Paradise Lost,* Book IV.
[40]*Argus:* In Greek mythology, a many-eyed monster.

times a night. A mirror (let us be elegant!) of the dimensions of a muf-
fin, and about as reflective, hung over a tin basin, blue pitcher, and a
brace of yellow mugs. Two invalid tables, ditto chairs, wandered here
and there, and the closet contained a varied collection of bonnets,
bottles, bags, boots, bread and butter, boxes and bugs. The closet was
a regular Blue Beard cupboard to me; I always opened it with fear and
trembling, owing to rats, and shut it in anguish of spirit; for time and
space were not to be had, and chaos reigned along with the rats. Our
chimney-piece was decorated with a flat-iron, a Bible, a candle minus
stick, a lavender bottle, a new tin pan, so brilliant that it served nicely
for a pier-glass, and such of the portly black bugs as preferred a
warmer climate than the rubbish hole afforded. Two arks, commonly
called trunks, lurked behind the door, containing the worldly goods of
the twain who laughed and cried, slept and scrambled, in this refuge;
while from the white-washed walls above either bed, looked down the
pictured faces of those whose memory can make for us—

"One little room an everywhere."[41]

For a day or two I managed to appear at meals; for the human grub
must eat till the butterfly is ready to break loose, and no one had time
to come up two flights while it was possible for me to come down. Far
be it from me to add another affliction or reproach to that enduring
man, the steward; for, compared with his predecessor, he was a horn
of plenty; but—I put it to any candid mind—is not the following bill of
fare susceptible of improvement, without plunging the nation madly
into debt? The three meals were "pretty much of a muchness," and
consisted of beef, evidently put down for the men of '76; pork, just in
from the street; army bread, composed of saw-dust and saleratus;[42]
butter, salt as if churned by Lot's wife;[43] stewed blackberries, so much
like preserved cockroaches, that only those devoid of imagination
could partake thereof with relish; coffee, mild and muddy; tea, three
dried huckleberry leaves to a quart of water—flavored with lime—
also animated and unconscious of any approach to clearness. Variety
being the spice of life, a small pinch of the article would have been
appreciated by the hungry, hard-working sisterhood, one of whom,
though accustomed to plain fare, soon found herself reduced to bread

[41]A quotation from the poem "The Good-Morrow" by John Donne (1572–1631): "For
love, all love of other sights controls, / And makes one little room, an everywhere."

[42]*saleratus:* Another name for sodium bicarbonate, used in baking powder.

[43]*Lot's wife:* In the biblical story of Lot's wife, Lot escaped the destruction of Sodom,
but his wife was turned into a pillar of salt for looking back as they fled.

and water; having an inborn repugnance to the fat of the land, and the salt of the earth.[44]

Another peculiarity of these hospital meals was the rapidity with which the edibles vanished, and the impossibility of getting a drop or crumb after the usual time. At the first ring of the bell, a general stampede took place; some twenty hungry souls rushed to the dining-room, swept over the table like a swarm of locusts, and left no fragment for any tardy creature who arrived fifteen minutes late. Thinking it of more importance that the patients should be well and comfortably fed, I took my time about my own meals for the first day or two after I came, but was speedily enlightened by Isaac, the black waiter, who bore with me a few times, and then informed me, looking as stern as fate:

"I say, mam, ef you comes so late you can't have no vittles, — 'cause I'm 'bleeged fer ter git things ready fer de doctors 'mazin' spry arter you nusses and folks is done. De gen'lemen don't kere fer ter wait, no more does I; so you jes' please ter come at de time, and dere won't be no frettin' nowheres."

It was a new sensation to stand looking at a full table, painfully conscious of one of the vacuums which Nature abhors, and receive orders to right about face, without partaking of the nourishment which your inner woman clamorously demanded. The doctors always fared better than we; and for a moment a desperate impulse prompted me to give them a hint, by walking off with the mutton, or confiscating the pie. But Ike's eye was on me, and, to my shame be it spoken, I walked meekly away; went dinnerless that day, and that evening went to market, laying in a small stock of crackers, cheese and apples, that my boys might not be neglected, nor myself obliged to bolt solid and liquid dyspepsias, or starve. This plan would have succeeded admirably had not the evil star under which I was born, been in the ascendant during that month, and cast its malign influences even into my "'umble" larder; for the rats had their dessert off my cheese, the bugs set up housekeeping in my cracker-bag, and the apples like all worldly riches, took to themselves wings and flew away; whither no man could tell, though certain black imps might have thrown light upon the matter, had not the plaintiff in the case been loth to add another to the many trials of long-suffering Africa. After this failure I resigned myself to fate, and, remembering that bread was called the staff of life, leaned pretty exclusively upon it; but it proved a broken reed, and I came to

[44]Alcott was a vegetarian.

the ground after a few weeks of prison fare, varied by an occasional potato or surreptitious sip of milk.

Very soon after leaving the care of my ward, I discovered that I had no appetite, and cut the bread and butter interests almost entirely, trying the exercise and sun cure instead. Flattering myself that I had plenty of time, and could see all that was to be seen, so far as a lone lorn female[45] could venture in a city, one-half of whose male population seemed to be taking the other half to the guard house,—every morning I took a brisk run in one direction or another; for the January days were as mild as Spring. A rollicking north wind and occasional snow storm would have been more to my taste, for the one would have braced and refreshed tired body and soul, the other have purified the air, and spread a clean coverlid over the bed, wherein the capital of these United States appeared to be dozing pretty soundly just then.

One of these trips was to the Armory Hospital, the neatness, comfort, and convenience of which makes it an honor to its presiding genius, and arouses all the covetous propensities of such nurses as came from other hospitals to visit it.

The long, clean, warm, and airy wards, built barrack-fashion, with the nurse's room at the end, were fully appreciated by Nurse Periwinkle, whose ward and private bower were cold, dirty, inconvenient, up stairs and down stairs, and in everybody's chamber. At the Armory, in ward K, I found a cheery, bright-eyed, white-aproned little lady, reading at her post near the stove; matting under her feet; a draft of fresh air flowing in above her head; a table full of trays, glasses, and such matters, on one side, a large, well-stocked medicine chest on the other; and all her duty seemed to be going about now and then to give doses, issue orders, which well-trained attendants executed, and pet, advise, or comfort Tom, Dick, or Harry, as she found best. As I watched the proceedings, I recalled my own tribulations, and contrasted the two hospitals in a way that would have caused my summary dismissal, could it have been reported at headquarters. Here, order, method, common sense and liberality reigned and ruled, in a style that did one's heart good to see; at the Hurly-burly Hotel, disorder, discomfort, bad management, and no visible head, reduced things to a condition which I despair of describing. The circumlocution fashion prevailed, forms and fusses tormented our souls, and unnecessary strictness in one place was counterbalanced by unpardonable laxity in

---

[45]*a lone lorn female:* Alcott quotes from Dickens's *David Copperfield,* in which Mrs. Gummidge repeatedly refers to herself as a "lone lorn creetur."

another. Here is a sample: I am dressing Sam Dammer's shoulder; and, having cleansed the wound, look about for some strips of adhesive plaster to hold on the little square of wet linen which is to cover the gunshot wound; the case is not in the tray; Frank, the sleepy, half-sick attendant, knows nothing of it; we rummage high and low; Sam is tired, and fumes; Frank dawdles and yawns; the men advise and laugh at the flurry; I feel like a boiling tea-kettle, with the lid ready to fly off and damage somebody.

"Go and borrow some from the next ward, and spend the rest of the day in finding ours," I finally command. A pause; then Frank scuffles back with the message: "Miss Peppercorn ain't got none, and says you ain't no business to lose your own duds and go borrowin' other folkses." I say nothing, for fear of saying too much, but fly to the surgery. Mr. Toddypestle informs me that I can't have anything without an order from the surgeon of my ward. Great heavens! where is he? and away I rush, up and down, here and there, till at last I find him, in a state of bliss over a complicated amputation, in the fourth story. I make my demand; he answers: "In five minutes," and works away, with his head upside down, as he ties an artery, saws a bone, or does a little needle-work, with a visible relish and very sanguinary pair of hands. The five minutes grow to fifteen, and Frank appears, with the remark that, "Dammer wants to know what in thunder you are keeping him there with his finger on a wet rag for?" Dr. P. tears himself away long enough to scribble the order, with which I plunge downward to the surgery again, find the door locked, and, while hammering away on it, am told that two friends are waiting to see me in the hall. The matron being away, her parlor is locked, and there is no where to see my guests but in my own room, and no time to enjoy them till the plaster is found. I settle this matter, and circulate through the house to find Toddypestle, who has no right to leave the surgery till night. He is discovered in the dead house, smoking a cigar, and very much the worse for his researches among the spirituous preparations that fill the surgery shelves. He is inclined to be gallant, and puts the finishing blow to the fire of my wrath; for the tea-kettle lid flies off, and driving him before me to his post, I fling down the order, take what I choose; and, leaving the absurd incapable kissing his hand to me, depart, feeling as Grandma Riglesty is reported to have done, when she vainly sought for chips, in Bimleck Jackwood's "shif'less paster."[46]

---

[46]*Grandma Riglesty, Bimleck Jackwood:* Characters in John Townsend Trowbridge's popular 1857 antislavery novel, *Neighbor Jackwood.*

I find Dammer a well acted charade of his own name, and, just as I get him done, struggling the while with a burning desire to clap an adhesive strip across his mouth, full of heaven-defying oaths, Frank takes up his boot to put it on, and explains:

"I'm blest ef here ain't the case now! I recollect seeing it pitch in this mornin', but forgot all about it, till my heel went smash inter it. Here, ma'am, ketch hold on it, and give the boys a sheet on't all round, 'gainst it tumbles inter t'other boot next time yer want it."

If a look could annihilate, Francis Saucebox would have ceased to exist, but it couldn't; therefore, he yet lives, to aggravate some unhappy woman's soul, and wax fat in some equally congenial situation.

Now, while I'm freeing my mind, I should like to enter my protest against employing convalescents as attendants, instead of strong, properly trained, and cheerful men. How it may be in other places I cannot say; but here it was a source of constant trouble and confusion, these feeble, ignorant men trying to sweep, scrub, lift, and wait upon their sicker comrades. One, with a diseased heart, was expected to run up and down stairs, carry heavy trays, and move helpless men; he tried it, and grew rapidly worse than when he first came: and, when he was ordered out to march away to the convalescent hospital, fell, in a sort of fit, before he turned the corner, and was brought back to die. Another, hurt by a fall from his horse, endeavored to do his duty, but failed entirely, and the wrath of the ward master fell upon the nurse, who must either scrub the rooms herself, or take the lecture; for the boy looked stout and well, and the master never happened to see him turn white with pain, or hear him groan in his sleep when an involuntary motion strained his poor back. Constant complaints were being made of incompetent attendants, and some dozen women did double duty, and then were blamed for breaking down. If any hospital director fancies this a good and economical arrangement, allow one used up nurse to tell him it isn't, and beg him to spare the sisterhood, who sometimes, in their sympathy, forget that they are mortal, and run the risk of being made immortal, sooner than is agreeable to their partial friends.

Another of my few rambles took me to the Senate Chamber, hoping to hear and see if this large machine was run any better than some small ones I knew of. I was too late, and found the Speaker's chair occupied by a colored gentleman of ten; while two others were "on their legs," having a hot debate on the cornball question,[47] as they gathered the waste paper strewn about the floor into bags; and several

[47]Cornballs were made of popcorn and molasses.

white members played leap-frog over the desks, a much wholesomer relaxation than some of the older Senators indulge in, I fancy. Finding the coast clear, I likewise gambolled up and down, from gallery to gallery; sat in Sumner's chair, and cudgelled an imaginary Brooks within an inch of his life;[48] examined Wilson's books in the coolest possible manner; warmed my feet at one of the national registers; read people's names on scattered envelopes, and pocketed a castaway autograph or two; watched the somewhat unparliamentary proceedings going on about me, and wondered who in the world all the sedate gentlemen were, who kept popping out of odd doors here and there, like respectable Jacks-in-the-box. Then I wandered over the "palatial residence" of Mrs. Columbia,[49] and examined its many beauties, though I can't say I thought her a tidy housekeeper, and didn't admire her taste in pictures, for the eye of this humble individual soon wearied of expiring patriots, who all appeared to be quitting their earthly tabernacles in convulsions, ruffled shirts, and a whirl of torn banners, bomb shells, and buff and blue arms and legs. The statuary also was massive and concrete, but rather wearying to examine; for the colossal ladies and gentlemen, carried no cards of introduction in face or figure; so, whether the meditative party in a kilt, with well-developed legs, shoes like army slippers, and a ponderous nose was Columbus, Cato, or Cockelorum Tibby, the tragedian,[50] was more than I could tell. Several robust ladies attracted me, as I felt particularly "wimbly" myself, as old country women say; but which was American and which Pocahontas was a mystery, for all affected much looseness of costume, dishevelment of hair, swords, arrows, lances, scales, and other ornaments quite *passé* with damsels of our day, whose effigies should go down to posterity armed with fans, crochet needles, riding whips, and parasols, with here and there one holding pen or pencil, rolling-pin or broom. The statue of Liberty[51] I recognized at once, for it had

[48]On May 22, 1856, Senator Charles Sumner of Massachusetts was physically attacked and seriously injured by Representative Preston Brooks of South Carolina on the floor of the U.S. Senate. A few days earlier, Sumner had made a speech harshly critical of slavery and of Senator Andrew Butler of South Carolina, Brooks's uncle.

[49]The Capitol.

[50]Alcott makes the joke that she can't tell whether the statues are of the famous explorer Columbus, the great Roman statesman and orator Cato, or an actor whose name she invents here. *Cockelorum* refers to someone with an unduly high opinion of himself.

[51]*Statue of Liberty:* The dome of the Capitol Building in Washington was unfinished at the beginning of the war. The Statue of Liberty, or Freedom, as it is known today, was put in place on the top of the dome on December 2, 1863.

no pedestal as yet, but stood flat in the mud, with Young America most symbolically making dirt pies, and chip forts, in its shadow. But high above the squabbling little throng and their petty plans, the sun shone full on Liberty's broad forehead, and, in her hand, some summer bird had built its nest. I accepted the good omen then, and, on the first of January, the Emancipation Act[52] gave the statue a nobler and more enduring pedestal than any marble or granite ever carved and quarried by human hands.

One trip to Georgetown Heights, where cedars sighed overhead, dead leaves rustled underfoot, pleasant paths led up and down, and a brook wound like a silver snake by the blackened ruins of some French Minister's house, through the poor gardens of the black washerwomen who congregated there, and, passing the cemetery with a murmurous lullaby, rolled away to pay its little tribute to the river. This breezy run was the last I took; for, on the morrow, came rain and wind: and confinement soon proved a powerful reinforcement to the enemy, who was quietly preparing to spring a mine, and blow me five hundred miles from the position I had taken in what I called my Chickahominy Swamp.[53]

Shut up in my room, with no voice, spirits, or books, that week was not a holiday, by any means. Finding meals a humbug, I stopped away altogether, trusting that if this sparrow was of any worth, the Lord would not let it fall to the ground. Like a flock of friendly ravens, my sister nurses fed me, not only with food for the body, but kind words for the mind; and soon, from being half starved, I found myself so beteaed and betoasted, petted and served, that I was quite "in the lap of luxury," in spite of cough, headache, a painful consciousness of my pleura, and a realizing sense of bones in the human frame. From the pleasant house on the hill, the home in the heart of Washington, and the Willard caravansary,[54] came friends new and old, with bottles,

[52] *Emancipation Act:* On New Year's Day in 1863, President Abraham Lincoln signed the Emancipation Proclamation, which declared freedom for slaves in rebellious states and also authorized the enlistment of former slaves in the Union Army. Despite the limited immediate impact of the proclamation (it did not actually free any slaves, as it affected only states still in rebellion against the United States), it was nevertheless widely understood to transform the conflict into a crusade against slavery rather than simply a war to preserve the union. For Alcott's reactions to the Emancipation Proclamation on January 1, 1863, see page 106.

[53] *Chickahominy Swamp:* Much of Union General George B. McClellan's March–July 1862 Peninsula Campaign in northern Virginia occurred near the Chickahominy River and its swamps.

[54] *Willard caravansary:* The Willard Hotel was the most important hotel in Washington during the Civil War.

baskets, carriages and invitations for the invalid; and daily our Florence Nightingale[55] climbed the steep stairs, stealing a moment from her busy life, to watch over the stranger, of whom she was as thoughtfully tender as any mother. Long may she wave! Whatever others may think or say, Nurse Periwinkle is forever grateful; and among her relics of that Washington defeat, none is more valued than the little book which appeared on her pillow, one dreary day; for the D. D. written in it means to her far more than Doctor of Divinity.[56]

Being forbidden to meddle with fleshly arms and legs, I solaced myself by mending cotton ones, and, as I sat sewing at my window, watched the moving panorama that passed below; amusing myself with taking notes of the most striking figures in it. Long trains of army wagons kept up a perpetual rumble from morning till night; ambulances rattled to and fro with busy surgeons, nurses taking an airing, or convalescents going in parties to be fitted to artificial limbs. Strings of sorry looking horses passed, saying as plainly as dumb creatures could, "Why, in a city full of them, is there no *horse*pital for us?" Often a cart came by, with several rough coffins in it, and no mourners following; barouches, with invalid officers, rolled round the corner, and carriage loads of pretty children, with black coachmen, footmen, and maids. The women who took their walks abroad, were so extinguished in three story bonnets, with overhanging balconies of flowers, that their charms were obscured; and all I can say of them is, that they dressed in the worst possible taste, and walked like ducks.

The men did the picturesque, and did it so well that Washington looked like a mammoth masquerade. Spanish hats, scarlet lined riding cloaks, swords and sashes, high boots and bright spurs, beards and mustaches, which made plain faces comely, and comely faces heroic; these vanities of the flesh transformed our butchers, bakers, and candlestick makers into gallant riders of gaily caparisoned horses, much handsomer than themselves; and dozens of such figures were constantly prancing by, with private prickings of spurs, for the benefit of the perambulating flower-bed. Some of these gentlemen affected painfully tight uniforms, and little caps, kept on by some new law of gravitation, as they covered only the bridge of the nose, yet never fell off; the men looked like stuffed fowls, and rode as if the safety of the

---

[55]*Florence Nightingale:* The famous English nurse (1820–1910) who revolutionized nursing during the Crimean War from 1854–56 and in 1860 founded the first professional school for nurses in London. (See the introduction.)

[56]*D. D.:* Alcott is referring to Dorothea Dix. (See the introduction.)

nation depended on their speed alone. The fattest, greyest officers dressed most, and ambled statelily along, with orderlies behind, trying to look as if they didn't know the stout party in front, and doing much caracoling on their own account.

The mules were my especial delight; and an hour's study of a constant succession of them introduced me to many of their characteristics; for six of these odd little beasts drew each army wagon, and went hopping like frogs through the stream of mud that gently rolled along the street. The coquettish mule had small feet, a nicely trimmed tassel of a tail, perked up ears, and seemed much given to little tosses of the head, affected skips and prances; and, if he wore the bells, or were bedizzened with a bit of finery, put on as many airs as any belle. The moral mule was a stout, hard-working creature, always tugging with all his might; often pulling away after the rest had stopped, laboring under the conscientious delusion that food for the entire army depended upon his private exertions. I respected this style of mule; and, had I possessed a juicy cabbage, would have pressed it upon him, with thanks for his excellent example. The historical mule was a melodramatic quadruped, prone to startling humanity by erratic leaps, and wild plunges, much shaking of his stubborn head, and lashing out of his vicious heels; now and then falling flat, and apparently dying *a la* Forrest:[57] a gasp—a squirm—a flop, and so on, till the street was well blocked up, the drivers all swearing like demons in bad hats, and the chief actor's circulation decidedly quickened by every variety of kick, cuff, jerk and haul. When the last breath seemed to have left his body, and "Doctors were in vain," a sudden resurrection took place; and if ever a mule laughed with scornful triumph, that was the beast, as he leisurely rose, gave a comfortable shake; and, calmly regarding the excited crowd seemed to say—"A hit! a decided hit! for the stupidest of animals has bamboozled a dozen men. Now, then! what are *you* stopping the way for?" The pathetic mule was, perhaps, the most interesting of all; for, though he always seemed to be the smallest, thinnest, weakest of the six, the postillion, with big boots, long-tailed coat, and heavy whip, was sure to bestride this one, who struggled feebly along, head down, coat muddy and rough, eye spiritless and sad, his very tail a mortified stump, and the whole beast a picture of meek misery, fit to touch a heart of stone. The jovial mule was a roly poly, happy-go-lucky little piece of horse-flesh, taking everything easily,

---

[57] *Forrest:* Edwin Forrest (1806–1872) was a famous American actor and national idol known especially for his bold, forceful, and melodramatic style as a tragedian.

from cudgeling to caressing; strolling along with a roguish twinkle of the eye, and, if the thing were possible, would have had his hands in his pockets, and whistled as he went. If there ever chanced to be an apple core, a stray turnip, or wisp of hay, in the gutter, this Mark Tapley[58] was sure to find it, and none of his mates seemed to begrudge him his bite. I suspected this fellow was the peacemaker, confidant and friend of all the others, for he had a sort of "Cheer-up,-old-boy,-I'll-pull-you-through" look, which was exceedingly engaging.

Pigs also possessed attractions for me, never having had an opportunity of observing their graces of mind and manner, till I came to Washington, whose porcine citizens appeared to enjoy a larger liberty than many of its human ones. Stout, sedate looking pigs, hurried by each morning to their places of business, with a preoccupied air, and sonorous greeting to their friends. Genteel pigs, with an extra curl to their tails, promenaded in pairs, lunching here and there, like gentlemen of leisure. Rowdy pigs pushed the passers by off the side walk; tipsy pigs hiccoughed their version of "We wont go home till morning," from the gutter; and delicate young pigs tripped daintily through the mud, as if, like "Mrs. Peerybingle,"[59] they plumed themselves upon their ankles, and kept themselves particularly neat in point of stockings. Maternal pigs, with their interesting families, strolled by in the sun; and often the pink, baby-like squealers lay down for a nap, with a trust in Providence worthy of human imitation.

But more interesting than officers, ladies, mules, or pigs, were my colored brothers and sisters, because so unlike the respectable members of society I'd known in moral Boston.

Here was the genuine article—no, not the genuine article at all, we must go to Africa for that—but the sort of creatures generations of slavery have made them: obsequious, trickish, lazy and ignorant, yet kind-hearted, merry-tempered, quick to feel and accept the least token of the brotherly love which is slowly teaching the white hand to grasp the black, in this great struggle for the liberty of both the races.

Having been warned not to be too rampant on the subject of slavery, as secesh principles flourished even under the respectable nose of Father Abraham,[60] I had endeavored to walk discreetly, and curb my unruly member; looking about me with all my eyes, the while, and saving up the result of my observations for future use. I had not been there a week, before the neglected, devil-may care

[58]*Mark Tapley:* Servant to Martin Chuzzlewit in Dickens's *Martin Chuzzlewit.*
[59]*Mrs. Peerybingle:* A character in Dickens's 1845 *Cricket on the Hearth.*
[60]*Father Abraham:* President Lincoln.

expression in many of the faces about me, seemed an urgent appeal to leave nursing white bodies, and take some care for these black souls. Much as the lazy boys and saucy girls tormented me, I liked them, and found that any show of interest or friendliness brought out the better traits which live in the most degraded and forsaken of us all. I liked their cheerfulness, for the dreariest old hag, who scrubbed all day in that pestilential steam, gossipped and grinned all the way out, when night set her free from drudgery. The girls romped with their dusky sweethearts, or tossed their babies, with the tender pride that makes mother-love a beautifier to the homeliest face. The men and boys sang and whistled all day long; and often, as I held my watch, the silence of the night was sweetly broken by some chorus from the street, full of real melody, whether the song was of heaven, or of hoe-cakes; and, as I listened, I felt that we never should doubt nor despair concerning a race which, through such griefs and wrongs, still clings to this good gift, and seems to solace with it the patient hearts that wait and watch and hope until the end.

I expected to have to defend myself from accusations of a prejudice against color; but was surprised to find things just the other way, and daily shocked some neighbor by treating the blacks as I did the whites. The men *would* swear at the "darkies," would put two *gs* into negro, and scoff at the idea of any good coming from such trash. The nurses were willing to be served by the colored people, but seldom thanked them, never praised, and scarcely recognized them in the street; whereat the blood of two generations of abolitionists waxed hot in my veins, and, at the first opportunity, proclaimed itself, and asserted the right of free speech as doggedly as the irrepressible Folsom[61] herself.

Happening to catch up a funny little black baby, who was toddling about the nurses' kitchen, one day, when I went down to make a mess for some of my men, a Virginia woman standing by elevated her most prominent features, with a sniff of disapprobation, exclaiming:

"Gracious, Miss P.! how can you? I've been here six months, and never so much as touched the little toad with a poker."

"More shame for you, ma'am," responded Miss P.; and, with the natural perversity of a Yankee, followed up the blow by kissing "the toad," with ardor. His face was providentially as clean and shiny as if his mamma had just polished it up with a corner of her apron and a

---

[61] *Folsom:* Abigail Folsom is a little-known figure of the antislavery movement whose eccentric speaking style embarrassed leaders of the antislavery movement, such as William Lloyd Garrison.

drop from the tea-kettle spout, like old Aunt Chloe.[62] This rash act, and the anti-slavery lecture that followed, while one hand stirred gruel for sick America, and the other hugged baby Africa, did not produce the cheering result which I fondly expected; for my comrade henceforth regarded me as a dangerous fanatic, and my protegé nearly came to his death by insisting on swarming up stairs to my room, on all occasions, and being walked on like a little black spider.

I waited for New Year's day with more eagerness than I had ever known before; and, though it brought me no gift, I felt rich in the act of justice so tardily performed toward some of those about me. As the bells rung midnight, I electrified my room-mate by dancing out of bed, throwing up the window, and flapping my handkerchief, with a feeble cheer, in answer to the shout of a group of colored men in the street below. All night they tooted and tramped, fired crackers, sung "Glory, Hallelujah," and took comfort, poor souls! in their own way. The sky was clear, the moon shone benignly, a mild wind blew across the river, and all good omens seemed to usher in the dawn of the day whose noontide cannot now be long in coming. If the colored people had taken hands and danced around the White House, with a few cheers for the much abused gentleman who has immortalized himself by one just act, no President could have had a finer levee, or one to be prouder of.

While these sights and sounds were going on without, curious scenes were passing within, and I was learning that one of the best methods of fitting oneself to be a nurse in a hospital, is to be a patient there; for then only can one wholly realize what the men suffer and sigh for; how acts of kindness touch and win; how much or little we are to those about us; and for the first time really see that in coming there we have taken our lives in our hands, and may have to pay dearly for a brief experience. Every one was very kind; the attendants of my ward often came up to report progress, to fill my woodbox, or bring messages and presents from my boys. The nurses took many steps with those tired feet of theirs, and several came each evening, to chat over my fire and make things cosy for the night. The doctors paid daily visits, tapped at my lungs to see if pneumonia was within, left doses without names, and went away, leaving me as ignorant, and much more uncomfortable than when they came. Hours began to get

---

[62]*Aunt Chloe:* Uncle Tom's wife in Harriet Beecher Stowe's *Uncle Tom's Cabin.* In mentioning Aunt Chloe here, Alcott reveals that, like most white Northerners, she viewed African Americans through the lenses of racial stereotypes drawn from popular culture.

confused; people looked odd; queer faces haunted the room, and the nights were one long fight with weariness and pain. Letters from home grew anxious; the doctors lifted their eyebrows, and nodded ominously; friends said "Don't stay," and an internal rebellion seconded the advice; but the three months were not out, and the idea of giving up so soon was proclaiming a defeat before I was fairly routed; so to all "Don't stays" I opposed "I wills," till, one fine morning, a grey-headed gentlemen rose like a welcome ghost on my hearth; and, at the sight of him, my resolution melted away, my heart turned traitor to my boys, and, when he said, "Come home," I answered, "Yes, father;" and so ended my career as an army nurse.

I never shall regret the going, though a sharp tussle with typhoid; ten dollars, and a wig, are all the visible results of the experiment; for one may live and learn much in a month. A good fit of illness proves the value of health; real danger tries one's mettle; and self-sacrifice sweetens character. Let no one who sincerely desires to help the work on in this way, delay going through any fear; for the worth of life lies in the experiences that fill it, and this is one which cannot be forgotten. All that is best and bravest in the hearts of men and women, comes out in scenes like these; and, though a hospital is a rough school, its lessons are both stern and salutary; and the humblest of pupils there, in proportion to his faithfulness, learns a deeper faith in God and in himself. I, for one, would return tomorrow, on the "up-again,-and-take-another" principle, if I could; for the amount of pleasure and profit I got out of that month compensates for all after pangs; and, though a sadly womanish feeling, I take some satisfaction in the thought that, if I could not lay my head on the altar of my country, I have my hair; and that is more than handsome Helen[63] did for her dead husband, when she sacrificed only the ends of her ringlets on his urn. Therefore, I close this little chapter of hospital experiences, with the regret that they were no better worth recording; and add the poetical gem with which I consoled myself for the untimely demise of "Nurse Periwinkle:"

> Oh, lay her in a little pit,
> With a marble stone to cover it;
> And carve thereon a gruel spoon,
> To show a "nuss" has died too soon.[64]

[63] *Helen:* From Greek mythology. Helen was the cause of The Trojan War when Paris stole her away from her husband Menelaus.

[64] This is perhaps a gentle parody of an old Irish ballad, "The Butcher Boy," whose last verse reads, in part, "Oh make my grave, long wide and deep / with a marble stone at my head and feet."

## CHAPTER VI. A POSTSCRIPT

*My Dear S.:*—As inquiries like your own have come to me from various friendly readers of the Sketches, I will answer them *en masse,* and
in printed form, as a sort of postscript to what has gone before. One of
these questions was, "Are there no services by hospital death-beds, or
on Sundays?"

In most Hospitals I hope there are; in ours, the men died, and were
carried away, with as little ceremony as on a battlefield. The first event
of this kind which I witnessed was so very brief, and bare of anything
like reverence, sorrow, or pious consolation, that I heartily agreed
with the bluntly expressed opinion of a Maine man lying next his comrade, who died with no visible help near him, but a compassionate
woman and a tender-hearted Irishman, who dropped upon his knees,
and told his beads, with Catholic fervor, for the good of his Protestant
brother's parting soul:

"If, after gettin' all the hard knocks, we are left to die this way, with
nothing but a Paddy's prayers to help us, I guess Christians are rather
scarce round Washington."

I thought so too; but though Miss Blank, one of my mates, anxious
that souls should be ministered to, as well as bodies, spoke more than
once to the Chaplain, nothing ever came of it. Unlike another Shep-
herd, whose earnest piety weekly purified the Senate Chamber, this
man did not feed as well as fold his flock, nor make himself a human
symbol of the Divine Samaritan, who never passes by on the other
side.

I have since learned that our non-commital Chaplain had been a
Professor, in some Southern College; and, though he maintained that
he had no secesh proclivities, I can testify that he seceded from his
ministerial duties, I may say, skedaddled, for, being one of his own
words, it is as appropriate as inelegant. He read Emerson, quoted Carlyle,[65] and tried to be a Chaplain; but, judging from his success, I am
afraid he still hankered after the hominy pots of Rebeldom.

Occasionally, on a Sunday afternoon, such of the nurses, officers,
attendants, and patients as could avail themselves of it, were gathered
in the Ball Room, for an hour's service, of which the singing was the

---

[65]*Emerson, Carlyle:* Ralph Waldo Emerson (1803–1882), the great Transcendentalist
philosopher, was the author of such works as *Nature* (1833) and *The Conduct of Life*
(1860). Thomas Carlyle (1795–1881), the British essayist and historian, was the author
of *The French Revolution* (1837), among other works.

better part. To me it seemed that if ever strong, wise, and loving words were needed, it was then; if ever mortal man had living texts before his eyes to illustrate and illuminate his thought, it was there; and if ever hearts were prompted to devoutest self-abnegation, it was in the work which brought us to anything but a Chapel of Ease. But some spiritual paralysis seemed to have befallen our pastor; for, though many faces turned toward him, full of the dumb hunger that often comes to men when suffering or danger brings them nearer to the heart of things, they were offered the chaff of divinity, and its wheat was left for less needy gleaners, who knew where to look. Even the fine old Bible stories, which may be made as lifelike as any history of our day, by a vivid fancy and pictorial diction, were robbed of all their charms by dry explanations and literal applications, instead of being useful and pleasant lessons to those men, whom weakness had rendered as docile as children in a father's hands.

I watched the listless countenances all about me, while a mild Daniel was moralizing in a den of utterly uninteresting lions; while Shadrach, Meshech, and Abednego were leisurely passing through the fiery furnace, where, I sadly feared, some of us sincerely wished they had remained as permanencies; while the Temple of Solomon[66] was laboriously erected, with minute descriptions of the process, and any quantity of bells and pomegranates on the raiment of the priests. Listless they were at the beginning, and listless at the end; but the instant some stirring old hymn was given out, sleepy eyes brightened, lounging figures sat erect, and many a poor lad rose up in his bed, or stretched an eager hand for the book, while all broke out with a heartiness that proved that somewhere at the core of even the most abandoned, there still glowed some remnant of the native piety that flows in music from the heart of every little child. Even the big rebel joined, and boomed away in a thunderous bass, singing—

"Salvation! let the echoes fly,"

---

[66] *Daniel, Shadrach, Meshech, Abednego, Temple of Solomon:* Alcott refers to two stories from the Book of Daniel. In the first, Daniel is thrown into a den of lions for holding fast to his faith but is protected from harm by divine intervention. In the second, Shadrach, Meshech, and Abednego are miraculously delivered from death in a fiery furnace after refusing to worship a golden image set up by King Nebuchadnezzar of Babylon. Alcott also refers to the detailed descriptions of the building of the Temple of Solomon in First Kings and Second Chronicles, which include specifications of designs of pomegranates. Alcott makes two related jokes here: first, that the chaplain makes even the most exciting stories from the Bible dull; second, that he makes a "boring," detailed biblical passage even more boring.

as energetically as if he felt the need of a speedy execution of the command.

That was the pleasantest moment of the hour, for then it seemed a homelike and happy spot; the groups of men looking over one another's shoulders as they sang; the few silent figures in the beds; here and there a woman noiselessly performing some necessary duty, and singing as she worked; while in the arm chair standing in the midst, I placed, for my own satisfaction, the imaginary likeness of a certain faithful pastor, who took all outcasts by the hand, smote the devil in whatever guise he came, and comforted the indigent in spirit with the best wisdom of a great and tender heart, which still speaks to us from its Italian grave. With that addition, my picture was complete; and I often longed to take a veritable sketch of a Hospital Sunday, for, despite its drawbacks, consisting of continued labor, the want of proper books, the barren preaching that bore no fruit, this day was never like the other six.

True to their home training, our New England boys did their best to make it what it should be. With many, there was much reading of Testaments, humming over of favorite hymns, and looking at such books as I could cull from a miscellaneous library. Some lay idle, slept, or gossiped; yet, when I came to them for a quiet evening chat, they often talked freely and well of themselves; would blunder out some timid hope that their troubles might "do 'em good, and keep 'em stiddy;" would choke a little, as they said good night, and turned their faces to the wall to think of mother, wife, or home, these human ties seeming to be the most vital religion which they yet knew. I observed that some of them did not wear their caps on this day, though at other times they clung to them like Quakers; wearing them in bed, putting them on to read the paper, eat an apple, or write a letter, as if, like a new sort of Samson, their strength lay, not in their hair, but in their hats. Many read no novels, swore less, were more silent, orderly, and cheerful, as if the Lord were an invisible Wardmaster, who went his rounds but once a week, and must find all things at their best. I liked all this in the poor, rough boys, and could have found it in my heart to put down sponge and tea-pot, and preach a little sermon then and there, while homesickness and pain had made these natures soft, that some good seed might be cast therein, to blossom and bear fruit here or hereafter.

Regarding the admission of friends to nurse their sick, I can only say, it was not allowed at Hurlyburly House; though one indomitable parent took my ward by storm, and held her position, in spite of doctors, matron, and Nurse Periwinkle. Though it was against the rules, though the culprit was an acid, frost-bitten female, though the young man would have done quite as well without her anxious fussiness, and the whole room-full been much more comfortable, there was something so irresistible in this persistent devotion, that no one had the heart to oust her from her post. She slept on the floor, without uttering a complaint; bore jokes somewhat of the rudest; fared scantily, though her basket was daily filled with luxuries for her boy; and tended that petulant personage with a never-failing patience beautiful to see.

I feel a glow of moral rectitude in saying this of her; for, though a perfect pelican to her young, she pecked and cackled (I don't know that pelicans usually express their emotions in that manner,) most obstreperously, when others invaded her premises; and led me a weary life, with "George's tea-rusks," "George's foot-bath," "George's measles," and "George's mother;" till, after a sharp passage of arms and tongues with the matron, she wrathfully packed up her rusks, her son, and herself, and departed, in an ambulance, scolding to the very last.

This is the comic side of the matter. The serious one is harder to describe; for the presence, however brief, of relations and friends by the bedsides of the dead or dying, is always a trial to the bystanders. They are not near enough to know how best to comfort, yet too near to turn their backs upon the sorrow that finds its only solace in listening to recitals of last words, breathed into nurse's ears, or receiving the tender legacies of love and longing bequeathed through them.

To me, the saddest sight I saw in that sad place, was the spectacle of a grey-haired father, sitting hour after hour by his son, dying from the poison of his wound. The old father, hale and hearty; the young son, past all help, though one could scarcely believe it; for the subtle fever, burning his strength away, flushed his cheeks with color, filled his eyes with lustre, and lent a mournful mockery of health to face and figure, making the poor lad comelier in death than in life. His bed was not in my ward; but I was often in and out, and, for a day or two, the pair were much together, saying little, but looking much. The old man tried to busy himself with book or pen, that his presence might not be a burden; and once when he sat writing, to the anxious mother at home, doubtless, I saw the son's eyes fixed upon his face, with a look of mingled resignation and regret, as if endeavoring to teach himself to say cheerfully the long good bye. And again, when the son slept, the father watched him, as he had himself been watched; and though no feature of his grave countenance changed, the rough hand, smoothing the lock of hair upon the pillow, the bowed attitude of the grey head, were more pathetic than the loudest lamentations. The son died; and the father took home the pale relic of the life he gave, offering a little money to the nurse, as the only visible return it was in his power to make her; for, though very grateful, he was poor. Of course, she did not take it, but found a richer compensation in the old man's earnest declaration:

"My boy couldn't have been better cared for if he'd been at home; and God will reward you for it, though I can't."

My own experiences of this sort began when my first man died. He had scarcely been removed, when his wife came in. Her eye went straight to the well-known bed; it was empty; and feeling, yet not believing the hard truth, she cried out, with a look I never shall forget:

"Why, where's Emanuel?"

I had never seen her before, did not know her relationship to the man whom I had only nursed for a day, and was about to tell her he was gone, when McGee, the tender-hearted Irishman before mentioned, brushed by me with a cheerful—"It's shifted to a better bed he is, Mrs. Connel. Come out, dear, till I show ye;" and, taking her gently by the arm, he led her to the matron, who broke the heavy tidings to the wife, and comforted the widow.

Another day, running up to my room for a breath of fresh air and a five minutes' rest after a disagreeable task, I found a stout young woman sitting on my bed, wearing the miserable look which I had learned to know by that time. Seeing her, reminded me that I had heard of some one's dying in the night, and his sister's arriving in the morning. This must be she, I thought. I pitied her with all my heart. What could I say or do? Words always seem impertinent at such times; I did not know the man; the woman was neither interesting in herself nor graceful in her grief; yet, having known a sister's sorrow myself, I could not leave her alone with her trouble in that strange place, without a word. So, feeling heart-sick, home-sick, and not knowing what else to do, I just put my arms about her, and began to cry in a very helpless but hearty way; for, as I seldom indulge in this moist luxury, I like to enjoy it with all my might, when I do.

It so happened I could not have done a better thing; for, though not a word was spoken, each felt the other's sympathy; and, in the silence, our handkerchiefs were more eloquent than words. She soon sobbed herself quiet; and, leaving her on my bed, I went back to work, feeling much refreshed by the shower, though I'd forgotten to rest, and had washed my face instead of my hands. I mention this successful experiment as a receipt proved and approved, for the use of any nurse who may find herself called upon to minister to these wounds of the heart. They will find it more efficacious than cups of tea, smelling-bottles, psalms, or sermons; for a friendly touch and a companionable cry, unite the consolations of all the rest for womankind; and, if genuine, will be found a sovereign cure for the first sharp pang so many suffer in these heavy times.

I am gratified to find that my little Sergeant has found favor in several quarters, and gladly respond to sundry calls for news of him, though my personal knowledge ended five months ago. Next to my good John—I hope the grass is green above him, far away there in Virginia!—I placed the Sergeant on my list of worthy boys; and many a jovial chat have I enjoyed with the merry-hearted lad, who had a fancy for fun, when his poor arm was dressed. While Dr. P. poked and strapped, I brushed the remains of the Sergeant's brown mane— shorn sorely against his will—and gossiped with all my might, the boy making odd faces, exclamations, and appeals, when nerves got the better of nonsense, as they sometimes did:

"I'd rather laugh than cry, when I must sing out anyhow, so just say that bit from Dickens again, please, and I'll stand it like a man." He did; for "Mrs. Cluppins," "Chadband," and "Sam Weller,"[67] always helped him through; thereby causing me to lay another offering of love and admiration on the shrine of the god of my idolatry, though he does wear too much jewelry and talk slang.

The Sergeant also originated, I believe, the fashion of calling his neighbors by their afflictions instead of their names; and I was rather taken aback by hearing them bandy remarks of this sort, with perfect good humor and much enjoyment of the new game.

"Hallo, old Fits is off again!" "How are you, Rheumatiz?" "Will you trade apples, Ribs?" "I say, Miss P., may I give Typus a drink of this?" "Look here, No Toes, lend us a stamp, there's a good feller," etc. He himself was christened "Baby B.," because he tended his arm on a little pillow, and called it his infant.

Very fussy about his grub was Sergeant B., and much trotting of attendants was necessary when he partook of nourishment. Anything more irresistably wheedlesome I never saw, and constantly found

---

[67] *Mrs. Cluppins, Chadband, Sam Weller:* Mrs. Cluppins and Sam Weller are characters in Dickens's 1837 *Pickwick Papers;* Chadband is a character in Dickens's 1853 *Bleak House.*

myself indulging him, like the most weak-minded parent, merely for the pleasure of seeing his brown eyes twinkle, his merry mouth break into a smile, and his one hand execute a jaunty little salute that was entirely captivating. I am afraid that Nurse P. damaged her dignity, frolicking with this persuasive young gentleman, though done for his well-being. But "boys will be boys," is perfectly applicable to the case; for, in spite of years, sex, and the "prunes-and-prisms" doctrine laid down for our use, I have a fellow feeling for lads, and always owed Fate a grudge because I wasn't a lord of creation instead of a lady.

Since I left, I have heard, from a reliable source, that my Sergeant has gone home; therefore, the small romance that budded the first day I saw him, has blossomed into its second chapter; and I now imagine "dearest Jane" filling my place, tending the wounds I tended, brushing the curly jungle I brushed, loving the excellent little youth I loved, and eventually walking altarward, with the Sergeant stumping gallantly at her side. If she doesn't do all this, and no end more, I'll never forgive her; and sincerely pray to the guardian saint of lovers, that "Baby B." may prosper in his wooing, and his name be long in the land.

One of the lively episodes of hospital life, is the frequent marching away of such as are well enough to rejoin their regiments, or betake themselves to some convalescent camp. The ward master comes to the door of each room that is to be thinned, reads off a list of names, bids their owners look sharp and be ready when called for; and, as he vanishes, the rooms fall into an indescribable state of topsy-turvyness, as the boys begin to black their boots, brighten spurs, if they have them, overhaul knapsacks, make presents; are fitted out with needfuls, and—well, why not?—kissed sometimes, as they say, good by; for in all human probability we shall never meet again, and a woman's heart yearns over anything that has clung to her for help and comfort. I never liked these breakings-up of my little household; though my short stay showed me but three. I was immensely gratified by the hand shakes I got, for their somewhat painful cordiality assured me that I had not tried in vain. The big Prussian rumbled out his unintelligible *adieux,* with a grateful face and a premonitory smooth of his yellow moustache, but got no farther, for some one else stepped up, with a large brown hand extended, and this recommendation of our very faulty establishment:

"We're off, ma'am, and I'm powerful sorry, for I'd no idea a 'orspittle was such a jolly place. Hope I'll git another ball somewheres easy, so I'll come back, and be took care on again. Mean, ain't it?"

I didn't think so, but the doctrine of inglorious ease was not the right one to preach up, so I tried to look shocked, failed signally, and consoled myself by giving him the fat pincushion he had admired as the "cutest little machine agoin." Then they fell into line in front of the house, looking rather wan and feeble, some of them, but trying to step out smartly and march in good order, though half the knapsacks were carried by the guard, and several leaned on sticks instead of shouldering guns. All looked up and smiled, or waved their hands and touched their caps, as they passed under our windows down the long street, and so away, some to their homes in this world, and some to that in the next; and, for the rest of the day, I felt like Rachel[68] mourning for her children, when I saw the empty beds and missed the familiar faces.

You ask if nurses are obliged to witness amputations and such matters, as a part of their duty? I think not, unless they wish; for the patient is under the effects of ether, and needs no care but such as the surgeons can best give. Our work begins afterward, when the poor soul comes to himself, sick, faint, and wandering; full of strange pains and confused visions, of disagreeable sensations and sights. Then we must sooth and sustain, tend and watch; preaching and practicing patience, till sleep and time have restored courage and self-control.

I witnessed several operations; for the height of my ambition was to go to the front after a battle, and feeling that the sooner I inured myself to trying sights, the more useful I should be. Several of my mates shrunk from such things; for though the spirit was wholly willing, the flesh was inconveniently weak. One funereal lady came to try her powers as a nurse; but, a brief conversation eliciting the facts that she fainted at the sight of blood, was afraid to watch alone, couldn't possibly take care of delirious persons, was nervous about infections, and unable to bear much fatigue, she was mildly dismissed. I hope she found her sphere, but fancy a comfortable bandbox on a high shelf would best meet the requirements of her case.

Dr. Z. suggested that I should witness a dissection; but I never accepted his invitations, thinking that my nerves belonged to the living, not to the dead, and I had better finish my education as a nurse before I began that of a surgeon. But I never met the little man skipping through the hall, with oddly shaped cases in his hand, and an absorbed expression of countenance, without being sure that a select

---

[68]*Rachel:* A biblical reference to the Book of Jeremiah, in which Rachel weeps for her children.

party of surgeons were at work in the dead house, which idea was a rather trying one, when I knew the subject was some person whom I had nursed and cared for.

But this must not lead any one to suppose that the surgeons were willfully hard or cruel, though one of them remorsefully confided to me that he feared his profession blunted his sensibilities, and, perhaps, rendered him indifferent to the sight of pain.

I am inclined to think that in some cases it does; for, though a capital surgeon and a kindly man, Dr. P., through long acquaintance with many of the ills flesh is heir to, had acquired a somewhat trying habit of regarding a man and his wound as separate institutions, and seemed rather annoyed that the former should express any opinion upon the latter, or claim any right in it, while under his care. He had a way of twitching off a bandage, and giving a limb a comprehensive sort of clutch, which, though no doubt entirely scientific, was rather startling than soothing, and highly objectionable as a means of preparing nerves for any fresh trial. He also expected the patient to assist in small operations, as he considered them, and to restrain all demonstrations during the process.

"Here, my man, just hold it this way, while I look into it a bit," he said one day to Fitz G., putting a wounded arm into the keeping of a sound one, and proceeding to poke about among bits of bone and visible muscles, in a red and black chasm made by some infernal machine of the shot or shell description. Poor Fitz held on like grim Death, ashamed to show fear before a woman, till it grew more than he could bear in silence; and, after a few smothered groans, he looked at me imploringly, as if he said, "I wouldn't, ma'am, if I could help it," and fainted quietly away.

Dr. P. looked up, gave a compassionate sort of cluck, and poked away more busily than ever, with a nod at me and a brief—"Never mind; be so good as to hold this till I finish."

I obeyed, cherishing the while a strong desire to insinuate a few of his own disagreeable knives and scissors into him, and see how he liked it. A very disrespectful and ridiculous fancy, of course; for he was doing all that could be done, and the arm prospered finely in his hands. But the human mind is prone to prejudice; and, though a personable man, speaking French like a born "Parley voo," and whipping off legs like an animated guillotine, I must confess to a sense of relief when he was ordered elsewhere; and suspect that several of the men would have faced a rebel battery with less trepidation than they did Dr. P., when he came briskly in on his morning round.

As if to give us the pleasures of contrast, Dr. Z. succeeded him, who, I think, suffered more in giving pain than did his patients in enduring it; for he often paused to ask: "Do I hurt you?" and, seeing his solicitude, the boys invariably answered: "Not much; go ahead, Doctor," though the lips that uttered this amiable fib might be white with pain as they spoke. Over the dressing of some of the wounds, we used to carry on conversations upon subjects foreign to the work in hand, that the patient might forget himself in the charms of our discourse. Christmas eve was spent in this way; the Doctor strapping the little Sergeant's arm, I holding the lamp, while all three laughed and talked, as if anywhere but in a hospital ward; except when the chat was broken by a long-drawn "Oh!" from "Baby B.," an abrupt request from the Doctor to "Hold the lamp a little higher, please," or an encouraging, "Most through, Sergeant," from Nurse P.

The chief Surgeon, Dr. O., I was told, refused the higher salary, greater honor, and less labor, of an appointment to the Officer's Hospital, round the corner, that he might serve the poor fellows at Hurlyburly House, or go to the front, working there day and night, among the horrors that succeed the glories of a battle. I liked that so much, that the quiet, brown-eyed Doctor was my especial admiration; and when my own turn came, had more faith in him than in all the rest put together, although he did advise me to go home, and authorize the consumption of blue pills.

Speaking of the surgeons reminds me that, having found all manner of fault, it becomes me to celebrate the redeeming feature of Hurlyburly House. I had been prepared by the accounts of others, to expect much humiliation of spirit from the surgeons, and to be treated by them like a door-mat, a worm, or any other meek and lowly article, whose mission it is to be put down and walked upon; nurses being considered as mere servants, receiving the lowest pay, and, it's my private opinion, doing the hardest work of any part of the army, except the mules. Great, therefore, was my surprise, when I found myself treated with the utmost courtesy and kindness. Very soon my carefully prepared meekness was laid upon the shelf; and, going from one extreme to the other, I more than once expressed a difference of opinion regarding sundry messes it was my painful duty to administer.

As eight of us nurses chanced to be off duty at once, we had an excellent opportunity of trying the virtues of these gentlemen; and I am bound to say they stood the test admirably, as far as my personal observation went. Dr. O.'s stethoscope was unremitting in its attentions; Dr. S. brought his buttons into my room twice a day, with the regularity of a medical clock; while Dr. Z. filled my table with neat little bottles, which I never emptied, prescribed Browning, bedewed me with Cologne, and kept my fire going, as if, like the candles in St. Peter's, it must never be permitted to die out. Waking, one cold night, with the certainty that my last spark had pined away and died, and consequently hours of coughing were in store for me, I was much amazed to see a ruddy light dancing on the wall, a jolly blaze roaring up the chimney, and down upon his knees before it, Dr. Z., whittling shavings. I ought to have risen up and thanked him on the spot; but, knowing that he was one of those who like to do good by stealth, I only peeped at him as if he were a friendly ghost; till, having made things as cozy as the most motherly of nurses could have done, he crept away, leaving me to feel, as somebody says, "as if angels were a watching of me in my sleep;" though that species of wild fowl do not usually descend in broadcloth and glasses. I afterwards discovered that he split the wood himself on that cool January midnight, and went about making or mending fires for the poor old ladies in their dismal dens; thus causing himself to be felt—a bright and shining light in more ways than one. I never thanked him as I ought; therefore, I publicly make a note of it, and further aggravate that modest M. D. by saying that if this was not being the best of doctors and the gentlest of gentlemen, I shall be happy to see any improvement upon it.

To such as wish to know where these scenes took place, I must respectfully decline to answer; for Hurly-burly House has ceased to exist as a hospital; so let it rest, with all its sins upon its head,—perhaps I should say chimney top. When the nurses felt ill, the doctors departed, and the patients got well, I believe the concern gently faded from existence, or was merged into some other and better establishment, where I hope the washing of three hundred sick people is done out of the house, the food is eatable, and mortal women are not expected to possess an angelic exemption from all wants, and the endurance of truck horses.

Since the appearance of these hasty Sketches, I have heard from several of my comrades at the Hospital; and their approval assures me that I have not let sympathy and fancy run away with me, as that lively team is apt to do when harnessed to a pen. As no two persons see the same thing with the same eyes, my view of hospital life must be taken through my glass, and held for what it is worth. Certainly, nothing was set down in malice, and to the serious-minded party who objected to a tone of levity in some portions of the Sketches, I can only say that it is a part of my religion to look well after the cheerfulnesses of life, and let the dismals shift for themselves; believing, with good Sir Thomas More,[69] that it is wise to "be merrie in God."

The next hospital I enter will, I hope, be one for the colored regiments, as they seem to be proving their right to the admiration and kind offices of their white relations, who owe them so large a debt, a little part of which I shall be so proud to pay.

Yours,

With a firm faith

In the good time coming,[70]

T<small>RIBULATION</small> P<small>ERIWINKLE</small>.

[69] *Sir Thomas More:* The great English humanist and also chancellor of England, beheaded in 1535 for refusing to accept Henry VIII as head of the Church of England.

[70] One of the most popular songs of antebellum America was Stephen Foster's 1846 "There's a Good Time Coming."

# A Chronology of Louisa May Alcott's Life (1830–1888)

1830    Bronson Alcott and Abigail May are married.

1831    Anna Bronson Alcott is born.

1832    Louisa May Alcott is born in Germantown, Pennsylvania, on November 29.

1835    Elizabeth Sewall Alcott is born.

1840    Abby May Alcott is born.

1843    The Alcotts move to Fruitlands to begin a utopian experiment in communal living.

1857    The Alcotts purchase a house in Concord, Massachusetts.

1858    Elizabeth Alcott (Lizzie) dies.

1859    Bronson Alcott is appointed Concord's superintendent of schools.

1860    Anna is married to John Pratt in Concord. Louisa writes *Moods*.

1861    The Civil War begins with the firing on Fort Sumter on April 12. On July 21, the Union sustains a major defeat at Bull Run. On September 11, President Lincoln revokes General John C. Fremont's unauthorized military proclamation of emancipation in Missouri.

1862    In Tennessee, Ulysses S. Grant captures Fort Henry on February 6 and then captures Fort Donelson ten days later. On April 6–7, the Battle of Shiloh on the Tennessee River results in massive Union casualties. From June 25 to July 1, the Seven Days Battles near Richmond result in heavy losses for both armies. The Second Battle of Bull Run on August 29–30 results once again in Union retreat. On September 17, the Battle of Antietam is the bloodiest single day in U.S. military history. Proclaimed a Union victory, Antietam allows President Lincoln to issue his Preliminary Emancipation Proclamation. In November, Louisa applies for a position as a nurse in Washington. She takes up a position at the Union Hotel Hospital in Georgetown in December, on the eve of the arrival of wounded soldiers from the Battle of Fredericksburg on December 13.

**1863**    The Emancipation Proclamation takes effect on January 1, 1863, while Louisa is serving as a nurse in Washington. On January 7, Louisa becomes seriously ill. On January 16, Bronson arrives in Georgetown. On January 24, Bronson and Louisa depart Georgetown for Concord. Louisa cannot leave her room until March 22. After recovering, Louisa writes *Hospital Sketches,* which appears as a serial in the *Commonwealth* from May to June and then as a book in August. The Battle of Gettysburg takes place from July 1 to 3. On the Mississippi River, Vicksburg surrenders to Grant on July 4. In November, Alcott's "The Brothers" appears in the *Atlantic Monthly.* In December, she publishes *The Rose Family* (a fairy tale) and *On Picket Duty, and Other Tales* with James Redpath.

**1864**    Publishes "A Hospital Christmas" in the *Commonwealth* in two installments on January 8 and 15. Publishes a sketch called "The Hospital Lamp" in the February 24 and 25 issues of the *Daily Morning Drum-Beat,* a publication of the Brooklyn Sanitary Fair. Publishes an article titled "Colored Soldiers' Letters" in the July 1 *Commonwealth.* Publishes "Love and Loyalty" in the *United States Service Magazine* between July and December. In November, General William T. Sherman begins a March to the Sea in Georgia. Louisa publishes *Moods,* a novel for adults.

**1865**    The Civil War effectively ends with the surrender of General Robert E. Lee to Ulysses S. Grant at Appomattox Court House, Virginia, on April 9. Louisa travels to Europe in July.

**1867**    Edits *Merry's Museum,* a magazine for children.

**1868–**    Publishes *Little Women* with Roberts Brothers.
**1869**

**1869**    Reprints *Hospital Sketches* in a new volume titled *Hospital Sketches and Camp and Fireside Stories,* published by Roberts Brothers.

**1870**    Travels to Europe for the second time.

**1871**    Publishes *Little Men.*

**1873**    Publishes *Work,* her second novel for adults.

**1872–**    Publishes *Aunt Jo's Scrap-Bag* (six volumes).
**1882**

**1875**    Publishes *Eight Cousins.*

**1876**    Publishes *Rose in Bloom.*

**1878**    Publishes *Under the Lilacs.*

**1886**    Publishes *Jo's Boys.*

**1888**    Dies in Concord on March 6, two days after her father's death.

# Questions for Consideration

1. *Hospital Sketches* opens with a chapter detailing Nurse Periwinkle's (Alcott's) trials and tribulations in traveling to Washington to take up her job as hospital nurse. What do we learn about the expected private and public roles of women in the mid-nineteenth century from this account? What are the frustrations Alcott faces on her journey, and what causes them? What are her own concerns about appropriate behavior in public?

2. At the time of the Civil War, women could not vote, nor could they fight as soldiers. Why then does Alcott feel that she wants to contribute to the war effort? Does she feel that she is a full member of the nation? How would you characterize the nature of her patriotism?

3. How does Alcott justify her presence in the Union Hotel Hospital? What contribution does she claim she can make to the war effort?

4. Describe the hierarchy that exists in the hospital. Who works there? Who is at the top of the pecking order, and who is at the bottom? Where does Alcott situate herself within that hierarchy?

5. Judging from Alcott's account, were soldiers fortunate to be in a hospital like the Union Hotel Hospital, or was hospital medical care itself hazardous to soldiers' health? Assess the state of mid-nineteenth-century medicine based on Alcott's depiction of medical practices at the Union Hotel Hospital.

6. Does Alcott assume "sisterhood" with the other nurses at the Union Hotel Hospital? Are there limits to that sisterhood imposed by class and race?

7. Many commentators have noted the tender relationships among soldiers in *Hospital Sketches*. Are those loving friendships typical of wartime? What constitutes appropriate masculine and feminine behavior in wartime? How does war affect norms of femininity and masculinity?

8. How deeply committed to the Union cause are the soldiers for whom Alcott cares? Why? What do they understand that cause to be? Do they fight for the Union, for each other, or for other reasons?

9. The Civil War has been characterized as a home-front war that involved civilians as well as soldiers. What evidence of strong links between home front and battlefront can be found in *Hospital Sketches?* What roles do civilians play in Alcott's account?

10. The powerful centerpiece of *Hospital Sketches* is the chapter "A Night," which closes with the death of the noble soldier John. What about John makes him an emblem of ideal nationhood for Alcott? How does her relationship to John shift, and what does that show us about Alcott's own relationship to ideals of nationhood?

11. Throughout *Hospital Sketches,* Alcott claims maternal authority over her "brave boys." Why? Does calling soldiers her "children" mask sexual tension in the text? What does she gain by taking the role of "mother"?

12. What are the racial dynamics within the hospital? How are African Americans described in the text? Was Alcott, an abolitionist, committed to social equality with African Americans?

13. What role does humor play in Alcott's depictions of a "woman's war"? Why is humor so important to her? Does her humor undercut sentimentalism, or is it part of a sentimental approach? Does her humor allow her to be more critical of her surroundings?

14. Alcott wrote and published *Hospital Sketches* in the midst of war. Are there signs in the text that she may have censored her account for the sake of Union morale?

15. Does Alcott support reconciliation with the enemy? What is her attitude toward the Confederacy?

16. Alcott writes that Tribulation Periwinkle is a "woman's rights woman." How does this assertion play itself out in Alcott's life? Are there limits to her assertiveness? When is she deferential, and why?

17. On what grounds is Alcott critical of chaplains? Do you think her criticism is fair?

18. What rhetorical strategies does Alcott use to ingratiate herself with a Northern audience? In other words, how does *Hospital Sketches* work as a piece of writing? Analyze Alcott's diction and imagery. Does she offer "realistic" or "romantic" accounts of soldiers?

# Selected Bibliography

BY AND ABOUT LOUISA MAY ALCOTT AND THE ALCOTT FAMILY

Alcott, Bronson. *The Journals of Bronson Alcott.* Edited by Odell Shepard. Boston: Little, Brown, 1938.

Alcott, Bronson. *The Letters of A. Bronson Alcott.* Edited by Richard L. Herrnstadt. Ames: Iowa State University Press, 1969.

Alcott, Louisa May. *Alternative Alcott.* Edited by Elaine Showalter. New Brunswick, N.J.: Rutgers University Press, 1988.

Alcott, Louisa May. *Behind a Mask: The Unknown Thrillers of Louisa May Alcott.* Edited by Madeleine B. Stern. New York: William Morrow, 1975.

Alcott, Louisa May. *Freaks of Genius: Unknown Thrillers of Louisa May Alcott.* Edited by Daniel Shealy, Madeleine B. Stern, and Joel Myerson. New York: Greenwood Press, 1991.

Alcott, Louisa May. *Hospital Sketches.* Boston: James Redpath, 1863.

Alcott, Louisa May. *Hospital Sketches.* Edited by Bessie Z. Jones. Cambridge, Mass.: Belknap Press, 1960.

Alcott, Louisa May. *Hospital Sketches and Camp and Fireside Stories.* Boston: Roberts Brothers, 1869.

Alcott, Louisa May. *The Journals of Louisa May Alcott.* Edited by Joel Myerson, Daniel Shealy, and Madeleine B. Stern. Boston: Little, Brown, 1989.

Alcott, Louisa May. *Louisa May Alcott: Her Life, Letters, and Journals.* Edited by Ednah D. Cheney. Boston: Roberts Brothers, 1889.

Alcott, Louisa May. *Louisa May Alcott Unmasked: Collected Thrillers.* Edited by Madeleine B. Stern. Boston: Northeastern University Press, 1995.

Alcott, Louisa May. *Plots and Counterplots: More Unknown Thrillers of Louisa May Alcott.* Edited by Madeleine B. Stern. New York: William Morrow, 1976.

Alcott, Louisa May. *The Selected Letters of Louisa May Alcott.* Edited by Joel Myerson, Daniel Shealy, and Madeleine B. Stern. Boston: Little, Brown, 1987.

Barton, Cynthia H. *Transcendental Wife: The Life of Abigail May Alcott.* Lanham, Md.: University Press of America, 1996.

Bedell, Madelon. *The Alcotts: Biography of a Family.* New York: Clarkson N. Potter, 1980.

Brodhead, Richard H. *Cultures of Letters: Scenes of Reading and Writing in Nineteenth-Century America.* Chicago: University of Chicago Press, 1993.

Cheney, Ednah D. *Louisa May Alcott: Her Life, Letters, and Journals.* Boston: Roberts Brothers, 1889.

Dahlstrand, Frederick C. *Amos Bronson Alcott: An Intellectual Biography.* Rutherford, N.J.: Fairleigh Dickinson University Press, 1982.

Elbert, Sarah. *A Hunger for Home: Louisa May Alcott and Little Women.* Philadelphia: Temple University Press, 1984; rev. ed., New Brunswick, N.J.: Rutgers University Press, 1987.

Saxton, Martha. *Louisa May: A Modern Biography.* New York: Avon, 1978.

Shepard, Odell. *Pedlar's Progress: The Life of Bronson Alcott.* Boston: Little, Brown, 1937.

Stern, Madeleine B., ed. *Critical Essays on Louisa May Alcott.* Boston: G. K. Hall, 1984.

Stern, Madeleine B. *Louisa May Alcott.* Norman: University of Oklahoma Press, 1950.

CIVIL WAR NURSING

Austin, Anne. *The Woolsey Sisters of New York: A Family's Involvement in the Civil War and a New Profession.* Philadelphia: American Philosophical Society, 1971.

Bacon, Georgeanna Woolsey. *Three Weeks at Gettysburg.* New York: Anson D. F. Randolph, 1863.

Bacon, Georgeanna Woolsey, and Eliza Woolsey Howland. *My Heart toward Home: Letters of a Family during the Civil War.* 1899. Reprint, Roseville, Minn.: Edinborough Press, 2001.

Bacot, Ada W. *A Confederate Nurse: The Diary of Ada W. Bacot, 1860–1863.* Edited by Jean V. Berlin. Columbia: University of South Carolina Press, 1994.

Baker, Nina Brown. *Cyclone in Calico: The Story of Mary Ann Bickerdyke.* Boston: Little, Brown, 1952.

Brockett, L. P., and Mary C. Vaughan. *Woman's Work in the Civil War: A Record of Heroism, Patriotism, and Patience.* Philadelphia: Zeigler, McCurdy, 1868.

Bucklin, Sophronia E. *In Hospital and Camp: A Woman's Record of Thrilling Incidents among the Wounded in the Late War.* Philadelphia: John E. Potter, 1869.

Cummings, Kate. *Kate: The Journal of a Confederate Nurse.* Edited by Richard Barksdale Harwell. Baton Rouge: Louisiana State University Press, 1959.

Dannett, Sylvia G. L. *Noble Women of the North.* New York: T. Yoseloff, 1959.

Fraise, Richard J. *The Florence Nightingale of the Southern Army: Experiences of Mrs. Ella K. Newsom, Confederate Nurse in the Great War of 1861–1865.* New York: Broadway, 1914.

Gibbons, Abby Hopper. *Life of Abby Hopper Gibbons.* New York: G. P. Putnam's Sons, 1896.

Giesberg, Judith Ann. *Civil War Sisterhood: The U.S. Sanitary Commission and Women's Politics in Transition.* Boston: Northeastern University Press, 2000.

Gollaher, David. *Voice for the Mad: The Life of Dorothea Dix.* New York: Free Press, 1995.

Greenbie, Marjorie Barstow. *Lincoln's Daughters of Mercy.* New York: G. P. Putnam's Sons, 1944.

Hancock, Cornelia. *The South after Gettysburg.* Edited by Henrietta Shatton Jaquette. New York: Crowell, 1956.

Hoge, Mrs. A. H. *The Boys in Blue; Or, Heroes of the "Rank and File."* New York: E. B. Treat, 1867.

Holland, Mary Gardner. *Our Army Nurses.* Boston: B. Wilkins, 1895.

Leonard, Elizabeth. *Yankee Women: Gender Battles in the Civil War.* New York: Norton, 1994.

Livermore, Mary. *My Story of the War: A Woman's Narrative of Four Years Personal Experience as Nurse in the Union Army, and in Relief Work at Home, in Hospitals, Camps, and at the Front, during the War of the Rebellion.* Hartford, Conn.: A. D. Worthington, 1887.

Maher, Sister Mary Denis. *To Bind Up the Wounds of War: Catholic Sister Nurses in the U.S. Civil War.* Westport, Conn.: Greenwood Press, 1989.

Mason, Emily. "Memories of a Hospital Matron." *Atlantic Monthly* 90 (1902): 305–18, 475–85.

Massey, Mary Elizabeth. *Women in the Civil War.* 1966. Reprint, Lincoln: University of Nebraska Press, 1994. Originally titled *Bonnet Brigades.*

Moore, Frank, ed. *Women of the War: Their Heroism and Self-Sacrifice.* Hartford, Conn.: S. S. Scranton, 1867.

*Notes of Hospital Life from November, 1861 to August, 1863.* Philadelphia: J. B. Lippincott, 1864.

Oates, Stephen B. *A Woman of Valor: Clara Barton and the Civil War.* New York: Free Press, 1994.

Parsons, Emily Elizabeth. *Civil War Nursing: Memoir of Emily Elizabeth Parsons.* 1880. Reprint, New York: Garland, 1984.

Reed, William H. *Hospital Life in the Army of the Potomac.* 1866. Reprint, Boston: William Howell Reed, 1891.

Reverby, Susan. *Ordered to Care: The Dilemma of American Nursing, 1850–1945.* New York: Cambridge University Press, 1987.

Ropes, Hannah. *Civil War Nurse: The Diary and Letters of Hannah Ropes.* Edited by John R. Brumgardt. Knoxville: University of Tennessee Press, 1980.

Ross, Kristie. "Women Are Needed Here: Northern Protestant Women as Nurses during the Civil War, 1861–1865." Ph.D. diss., Columbia University, 1993.

Schultz, Jane E. "'Are We Not All Soldiers?' Northern Women in the Civil War Hospital Service." *Prospects* 20 (1995): 38–56.

Schultz, Jane E. "The Inhospitable Hospital: Gender and Professionalism in Civil War Medicine." *Signs* 17 (winter 1992): 363–92.

Schultz, Jane E. "Race, Gender, and Bureaucracy: Civil War Army Nurses and the Pension Bureau." *Journal of Women's History* 6 (summer 1994): 45–69.

Schultz, Jane E. "Seldom Thanked, Never Praised, and Scarcely Recognized: Gender and Racism in Civil War Hospitals" *Civil War History* 48 (September 2002): 220–36.

Smith, Adelaide W. *Reminiscences of an Army Nurse during the Civil War.* New York: Greaves Publishing Co., 1911.

Smith, Nina Bennett. "The Women Who Went to the War: The Union Army Nurse in the Civil War." Ph.D. diss., Northwestern University, 1981.

Stearns, Amanda Akin. *The Lady Nurse of Ward E.* New York: Baker and Taylor, 1909.

Taylor, Susie King. *Reminiscences of My Life: A Black Woman's Civil War Memoirs.* Edited by Patricia W. Romero and Willie Lee Rose. 1902. Reprint, New York: Marcus Wiener, 1988.

Wittenmyer, Annie. *Under the Guns: A Woman's Reminiscences of the Civil War.* Boston: E. B. Stillings, 1895.

Wood, Ann Douglas. "The War within a War: Women Nurses in the Union Army." *Civil War History* 18 (Sept. 1972): 191–212.

Woolsey, Jane Stuart. *Hospital Days: Reminiscence of a Civil War Nurse.* 1868. Reprint, Roseville, Minn.: Edinborough Press, 1996.

Wormeley, Katherine Prescott. *The Other Side of the War with the Army of the Potomac.* Boston: Ticknor, 1889.

Young, Agatha. *The Women and the Crisis: Women of the North in the Civil War.* New York: McDowell, Bolensky, 1959.

CIVIL WAR MEDICINE

Adams, George Worthington. *Doctors in Blue: The Medical History of the Union Army in the Civil War.* 1952. Reprint, New York: Collier, 1961.

Brinton, John H. *Personal Memoirs of John H. Brinton: Major and Surgeon, U.S.V., 1861–1865.* New York: Neale, 1914.

Brooks, Stewart. *Civil War Medicine.* Springfield, Ill.: Charles C. Thomas, 1966.

Confederate States of America, War Department. *Regulations for the Medical Department of the C.S. Army.* Richmond: Ritchie and Dunnavant, 1863.

Cunningham, Horace Herndon. *Doctors in Gray: The Confederate Medical Service.* Baton Rouge: Louisiana State University Press, 1958.

Denney, Robert E. *Civil War Medicine: Care and Comfort of the Wounded.* New York: Sterling, 1994.

Freemon, Frank R. *Gangrene and Glory: Medical Care during the American Civil War.* Madison, N.J.: Fairleigh Dickinson University Press, 1998.

Freemon, Frank R. *Microbes and Minie Balls: An Annotated Bibliography of Civil War Medicine.* Rutherford, N.J.: Fairleigh Dickinson University Press, 1993.

Steiner, Paul E. *Disease in the Civil War: Natural Biological Warfare in 1861–1865.* Springfield, Ill.: Charles C. Thomas, 1968.

Stille, Charles J. *History of the United States Sanitary Commission, Being the General Report of Its Work during the War of the Rebellion.* Philadelphia: J. B. Lippincott, 1866.

U.S. Sanitary Commission. *Surgical Memoirs of the War of the Rebellion.* 2 vols. New York: U.S. Sanitary Commission, 1870–1871.

U.S. Surgeon General's Office. *The Medical and Surgical History of the War of the Rebellion (1861–1865).* Washington, D.C.: Government Printing Office, 1875–1885.

Wilbur, C. Keith. *Civil War Medicine, 1861–1865.* Old Saybrook, Conn.: Globe Pequot Press, 1998.

WOMEN'S HISTORY AND THE CIVIL WAR

Attie, Jeanie. *Patriotic Toil: Northern Women and the American Civil War.* Ithaca, N.Y.: Cornell University Press, 1998.

Blanton, DeAnne, and Lauren M. Cook. *They Fought Like Demons: Women Soldiers in the American Civil War.* Baton Rouge: Louisiana State University Press, 2002.

Clinton, Catherine, and Nina Silber, eds. *Divided Houses: Gender and the Civil War.* New York: Oxford University Press, 1992.

Cott, Nancy. *The Bonds of Womanhood: "Woman's Sphere" in New England, 1780–1835.* New Haven, Conn.: Yale University Press, 1977.

Culpepper, Marilyn Mayer. *Trials and Triumphs: The Women of the American Civil War.* Lansing: Michigan State University Press, 1992.

DuBois, Ellen. *Feminism and Suffrage.* Ithaca, N.Y.: Cornell University Press, 1978.

Epstein, Barbara Leslie. *The Politics of Domesticity: Women, Evangelism, and Temperance in Nineteenth-Century America.* Middletown, Conn.: Wesleyan University Press, 1981.

Faust, Drew Gilpin. *Mothers of Invention: Women of the Slaveholding South in the American Civil War.* Chapel Hill: University of North Carolina Press, 1996.

Forbes, Ella. *African American Women during the Civil War.* New York: Garland, 1998.

Forten, Charlotte L. *The Journal of Charlotte L. Forten.* Edited by Ray Allen Billington. New York: Dryden Press, 1953.

Kelley, Mary. *Private Woman, Public Stage: Literary Domesticity in Nineteenth-Century America.* New York: Oxford University Press, 1984.

Kessler-Harris, Alice. *Out to Work: A History of Wage-Earning Women in the United States.* New York: Oxford University Press, 1982.

Leonard, Elizabeth D. *All the Daring of the Soldier: Women of the Civil War Armies.* New York: Norton, 1999.

Leonard, Elizabeth. *Yankee Women: Gender Battles in the Civil War.* New York: W. W. Norton, 1994.

Ryan, Mary. *Women in Public: Between Banners and Ballots, 1825–1880.* Baltimore: Johns Hopkins University Press, 1990.

Sizer, Lyde Cullen. *The Political Work of Northern Women Writers and the Civil War, 1850–1872.* Chapel Hill: University of North Carolina Press, 2000.

Wakeman, Sarah Rosetta. *An Uncommon Soldier: The Civil War Letters of Sarah Rosetta Wakeman, Alias Private Lyons Wakeman, 153rd Regiment, New York Volunteers, 1862–1864.* Edited by Lauren Cook Burgess. New York: Oxford University Press, 1995.

## THE CIVIL WAR

Berlin, Ira, Barbara J. Fields, Thavolia Glymph, Joseph P. Reidy, and Leslie S. Rowland, eds. *Freedom: A Documentary History of Emancipation, 1861–1867.* Ser. 1, vol. 1, *The Destruction of Slavery.* Cambridge: Cambridge University Press, 1985.

Fahs, Alice. *The Imagined Civil War: Popular Literature of the North and South, 1861–1865.* Chapel Hill: University of North Carolina Press, 2001.

Linderman, Gerald F. *Embattled Courage: The Experience of Combat in the American Civil War.* New York: Free Press, 1987.

McPherson, James M. *Battle Cry of Freedom: The Civil War Era.* New York: Oxford University Press, 1988.

McPherson, James M. *For Cause and Comrades: Why Men Fought in the Civil War.* New York: Oxford University Press, 1997.

McPherson, James M. *Ordeal by Fire: The Civil War and Reconstruction.* Rev. ed. New York: McGraw-Hill, 1992.

Mitchell, Reid. *Civil War Soldiers.* New York: Viking, 1988.

Mitchell, Reid. *The Vacant Chair: The Northern Soldier Leaves Home.* New York: Oxford University Press, 1993.

Paludan, Philip S. *A People's Contest: The Union and Civil War, 1861–1865.* New York: Harper & Row, 1988.

Rable, George C. *Fredericksburg! Fredericksburg!* Chapel Hill: University of North Carolina Press, 2002.

Rose, Anne C. *Victorian America and the Civil War.* Cambridge: Cambridge University Press, 1992.

Rose, Willie Lee. *Rehearsal for Reconstruction: The Port Royal Experiment.* 1964. Reprint, New York: Oxford University Press, 1976.

Royster, Charles. *The Destructive War: William Tecumseh Sherman, Stonewall Jackson, and the Americans.* New York: Knopf, 1991.

Stevenson, Louise L. *The Victorian Homefront: American Thought and Culture, 1860–1880.* New York: Twayne, 1991.

Sutherland, Donald E. *Fredericksburg and Chancellorsville: The Dare Mark Campaign.* Lincoln: University of Nebraska Press, 1998.

Wagner, Margaret E., Gary W. Gallagher, and Paul Finkelman, eds. *The Library of Congress Civil War Desk Reference.* New York: Simon & Schuster, 2002.

Wiley, Bell Irvin. *The Life of Billy Yank: The Common Soldier of the Union.* Indianapolis: Bobbs-Merrill, 1951; reprint, Baton Rouge: Louisiana State University Press, 1978.

Wiley, Bell Irvin. *The Life of Johnny Reb: The Common Soldier of the Confederacy.* Indianapolis: Bobbs-Merrill, 1943.

# Index

abolitionists, 41
African Americans. *See also* slavery
  attitudes toward, 41–42, 70*n*, 105–6
  "contraband," 13, 70
  descriptions of, 104–6
  employment of, 41
  infantilization of, 41
  portrayal of, 41
  regiments, 119
  Southern *vs.* Northern, 104
  women, 70*n*
"Against Idleness and Mischief" (Watts),
  61*n*
Alcott, Abba (Abigail May), 2, 3, 5, 120
Alcott, Abby May, 2, 120
Alcott, Anna, 2, 120
Alcott, Bronson, 3–4, 6, 28–29, 120, 121
Alcott, Elizabeth, 2, 120
Alcott, Louisa May. *See also* Nurse Periwinkle
  aid to freed slaves by, 14
  antislavery attitudes, 13–14
  born, 120
  charity work, 5
  chronology, 120–21
  Civil War interest of, 1, 13–14
  employment, 4–8, 31
  enters Army service, 18–20
  fame of, 30
  family, 2–4
  financial issues, 3–7
  gender roles and, 13, 35–38, 62
  *Hospital Sketches* written by, 29–32
  illness of, 28–29, 121
  leaves Army service, 28–29, 121
  letters about Army service, 29
  literary career, 1–2, 7–10, 30–32, 43
  literary style, 32–34
  men envied by, 11
  middle-class status, 5
  as nurse, 14–20
  racial attitudes, 41–42
  as seamstress, 6–7, 47*n*36
  as teacher, 6

  woman's suffrage and, 59*n*
  women's rights and, 59
  as writer, 7–10
Ambulance Corps, 23
ambulance system, 23
amputations, 115
anaesthesia, 25, 78
anonymous death, 38
antiwar Democrats, 74*n*
*Argus*, 94*n*
Armory Square Hospital, 20, 55*n*
  compared to Hurly-burly House, 55, 97
Army of the Potomac, 21
army wagons, 102–3
*Atlantic Monthly,* 7–8, 9, 15, 121
Aunt Chloe, 106*n*
*Aunt Jo's Scrap-Bag* (Alcott), 121

Baltimore, 66–67
Betsey Trotwood, 80*n*
Bickerdyke, Mary Ann, 28
Bimleck Jackwood, 98*n*
Blackwell, Elizabeth, 17
*Bleak House* (Dickens), 34, 113*n*
"blood and thunder" stories, 9–10
Book of Daniel, 109*n*
Book of Jeremiah, 115*n*
Boston, 57–62
boys, soldiers as, 37–38, 75
Brontë, Charlotte, 7
Brooks, Preston, 100*n*
"Brothers, The" (Alcott), 30, 121
Brown, John, 13–14, 30, 82*n*
Bull Run, Battle of, 11, 120
Bull Run, Second Battle of, 120
Bunyan, John, 60*n*
Burnside, Ambrose, 20, 21, 71*n*
"Butcher Boy, The," 107
Butler, Benjamin, 70*n*

camp fevers, 23
Carlyle, Thomas, 108*n*
Catholicism, 78*n*
Catholic Sisters of Charity, 17